LAID *in* CHELSEA

OLLIE LOCKE

LAID in CHELSEA

My Life Uncovered

HarperCollins*Publishers*

HarperCollins*Publishers*
77–85 Fulham Palace Road,
Hammersmith, London W6 8JB

www.harpercollins.co.uk

First published by HarperCollins*Publishers* 2013

1 3 5 7 9 10 8 6 4 2

A catalogue record of this book is
available from the British Library

ISBN 978-0-00-751395-6

Printed and bound in Great Britain by
Clays Ltd, St Ives plc

MIX
Paper from
responsible sources
FSC® C007454

FSC™ is a non-profit international organisation established to promote
the responsible management of the world's forests. Products carrying the
FSC label are independently certified to assure consumers that they come
from forests that are managed to meet the social, economic and
ecological needs of present and future generations,
and other controlled sources.

Find out more about HarperCollins and the environment at
www.harpercollins.co.uk/green

This book is dedicated to each and every incredible girl and guy included in this book who has changed and shaped my life and made me the person I am today.

Also to the city of London, my ultimate inspiration and the setting that housed so many of these relationships.

CONTENTS

MY GREATEST THANKS TO ...

My wonderful and beautiful family: Mum, Dad, Amelia and James, and the memory of a beautiful grandmother who, thank God, will never read this book. You are all my rock through everything, always.

Sarah Dillistone, and everyone involved in *Made in Chelsea*, for making everything possible and for changing my life.

My Cheska, Binky and Richard, and the rest of the cast, for sharing an unbelievable experience together.

My beautiful agents at Curtis Brown, Richard Gibb and Felicity Blunt, who save my life wherever I am in the world. Also, Jacquie, Jon, Gordon, Hannah, Becky and Fran for all being superstars.

My fabulous and beautiful editor Anna Valentine, who has the job of taking out all the REALLY naughty, unpublishable stories, and to everyone at HarperCollins who has made this book possible.

My best friends and one day best men at my wedding, Louis, Alex, Oscar and Richard, who have each made the last 26 years very amusing.

My wonderful Pink Palace urban family, Emily, Sam and George, for the wine, the parties, the shoulder. You are the three people I know will always be there.

Jordan, for everything, and for being my truly fabulous Bridget Jones.

Jason Holman, for driving me around the world and giving me all the relationship advice I need. You know everything before anyone else!

Jon and Matt at Insanity for all your help and support.

Luke, Ryan, Jamieson, Rollo and all my closest Chelsea friends who have shared the last seven years of truly wonderful memories after midnight.

FOREWORD

It's early October 2011. I'm sitting in my room surrounded by boxes of cigarettes and empty bottles of wine. It looks like a slum. My three flatmates are all out, and I have never felt so low in my entire life. I'm booked to do an appearance at a nightclub in Bristol tonight but I text saying I have been asked to film for *Made in Chelsea* so I can't make it. I have quite honestly cried for 72 hours. Looking in the mirror I think I look like I have lost everything. In some ways I feel that I have. My mum is calling every half an hour and I have hardly eaten in four days. My phone rings from an unknown number and I ignore it.

Two minutes later it rings again … and again. On the fourth time I pick up silently and listen.

'Your taxi is outside.'

I know I'm due on the *T4* sofa in 45 minutes to give an interview about the next series of *Made in Chelsea*. I have no choice – I have to go.

I put on any clothes I find that seem clean and I get into a large Mercedes with tinted windows. I sit in the back of the car, expressionless, while we make our way across London to a shopping centre in Bayswater.

When I walk into the TV studios I'm shown to a dressing room, where I cry into a bowl of Haribos. But I don't have time to dwell on my misery, as I'm quickly taken into another room, where I am covered in make-up to hide what I actually look like.

I then find myself standing on the edge of the set, waiting for my interview. I force myself to smile, knowing that I have to be on Ollie form for the next 20 minutes. I have to laugh and chat about how excited I am that filming for the next series is about to start. I have to be the Ollie from *Made in Chelsea* that everyone knows. But at that precise moment, I couldn't have felt any further from that. Inside I was dying and so far away from being Laid in Chelsea.

I had just gone through one of the hardest break-ups of my life. Whether *she* thought that way about it I don't know, but I felt as if I had lost everything.

* * *

Looking back at that moment now, I realise that no matter how bad it seems, no matter how bad the break-up, you can always bounce back. I'm now in a happy place – yes, I'm single and fairly sexless, but I believe in love, and I'd like to believe that the person I'm going to spend the rest of my life with is out there somewhere. It's only time that is holding back that moment when we will meet – probably when we're both least expecting it.

Of course, I've asked myself if there's such a thing as 'happily ever after'. We're supposed to believe it when we watch the great romantic Disney films, but who's to say what happens after the camera stops rolling? Maybe after *Beauty and the Beast* Belle realised she was terribly shallow and ran off in search of a better-looking man? Perhaps once Ariel from *The Little Mermaid* was on dry land she decided that it wasn't love she wanted, but a Ferrari and a credit card?

We all want to believe in love, but can we trust that we will end up with the right person, have three children and a Range Rover? Have we forgotten what love is all about? A house in the country and a wardrobe full of Sloane Street clothes is wonderful, but neither of these things will send you flowers for no reason, hug you when you've had a truly shit day, or handle morning-breath sex.

I want to bring back some of that belief in love, simply because I love the idea of being in love. In this book you will hear all about my life and my great loves – those that have helped make me into the person I am today, and those whose memory should definitely be taken and buried in the graveyard of failed romances and never spoken of again. But for now I'm happily digging them up to show that no matter how bad things get in the romance stakes, you should never give up hope that things *will* get better again. And, of course, I'll reveal all about those relationships that you may already be familiar with from a little show called *Made in Chelsea*.

During the 10 years I've been dating, I've had some amazing experiences and I have gathered a lot of stories along the way. Some are good; others are bad. Some loves have lasted hours, days, weeks or months, and some have stood firm for several years. I feel like the girls (and guys) I've dated have given me the equivalent of a doctorate in relationships, and I want to share what I've learned with you. So, light the candles, pour the champagne and prepare to get Laid in Chelsea …

CHAPTER 1
AND SO IT BEGINS …

Let's start way, way back, when I was a child. I grew up in Southampton and for the majority of my childhood I was the only boy in a household of females. My sister, Amelia, was two years older than me, which basically meant I was buying Tampax for toilet-stranded women from an early age. By the time I was 10 I'm fairly sure I could differentiate between 'medium' and 'super plus' using the box's colour codes.

I loved my sister, but to be honest I did always want an older brother. Amelia wasn't interested in digging up woodland creatures or playing conkers. She and my mum would always be in Marks & Spencer, with a chart to show which colours went best with her complexion while I played cars with the trolley. When I was about six, Mum was struggling to get the lid off a jar and I rolled my eyes and said, 'It was obviously designed by a man.' It was something I'd heard my mum say many times about various objects and I was probably trying to bond with her in the same way my sister did.

Because of my colouring, I often get asked about my heritage. So, to get the record straight, I have absolutely no idea why I'm so brown. My granddad on my mum's side was a chauffeur to the royals and was also Oscar Wilde's personal driver. He and my granny lived in a cottage in the Kensington Palace estate. My granddad on my dad's side made it possible for people to take long-haul flights. He invented a fireproof tank for planes that prevented them blowing up if there was a fire mid-flight. Mum's side of the family were never rich, whereas my dad's always drove Bentleys and were very wealthy.

Sadly, both of my grandfathers died before I was born, but I was very close to my grannies and they were wonderful women – one of them lived until she was 103 years old.

I definitely think spending so much time with my mum, sister and grannies gave me a better understanding of females. By 12 I knew what Touche Éclat was (it's make-up, lads) – at the time they only had one shade – and I'd also watch all of the girly movies of the day, tucked up on the sofa with my mum and Amelia. My upbringing also taught me from an early age how to show respect to women. I knew to stand nearest the cars when walking down the pavement with a woman, so if a car drove through a puddle I would get wet but they would be protected (at l east I think that's what we do it for!). It's so hard these days because if you want to give up your seat for a woman on the train they assume that you think they're pregnant, old or morbidly obese, but I'm determined that if I can find a way to be a gentleman that doesn't put me in danger of being beaten up by a large boyfriend and his dog, I will do it.

When I was around four years old I had my first crush. I can still remember it; I was at a wedding on the Caribbean island of St Lucia when I met a girl called Emma. She was beautiful, with blue eyes and long dark hair. She was the daughter of family friends who were getting married on the island that week. I thought she was perfect. I remember seeing her for the first time when we were both with our parents and I couldn't stop smiling at her. I probably looked like a right knob.

I must have been desperately trying to impress Emma, because I made the terrifically bad decision to make friends with the local kids and go and hang out on the beach with them in a bid to find a prize of a metaphorical slaughtered lamb for her.

After some Del-Boy-style negotiation (that may have looked like a very young drug deal), I ended up trading a pineapple I had pilfered from the wedding spread for a half-dead black and white sea snake. It was all they had to offer and it seemed like a great deal at the time.

When the speeches began I decided it was the perfect time to present my princess with her gift. I boldly marched into the reception dressed in my smartest clothes, smelling a little bit of dead snake and feeling very excited indeed. The best man was whipping out his comedy routine about the groom when I went straight to the top table and threw the snake onto the bride's plate. She recoiled in horror and the whole room went silent. Even worse, this whole scenario was played out in full view of Emma. Why I didn't attempt to hand it straight to Emma I'll never know, but I suspect it was because I wanted to cause the biggest commotion I could to get noticed by the object of my apparent desire. Needless to say, the entire party was soon in uproar.

The bride looked like she was going to have a seizure, and the only person who seemed even vaguely amused was my father, because he knew how much I would have enjoyed that moment.

I got into so much trouble afterwards that I temporarily forgot about my love for Emma. I was sent straight to bed by my mother, who was less than happy with my behaviour, and was robbed of the opportunity to roll about the dancefloor to cheesy songs as all kids love to do at weddings.

It was only when I woke up the next morning that I turned to my mum and said, 'Mummy, was she real?' because I thought I'd dreamed up both Emma and the snake. Mum had calmed down by then so she gave me a hug and told me that I would meet the right girl for me one day, and that I might need more time and a different approach to find her.

Needless to say I was ridiculed mercilessly by Amelia and I didn't get the girl either. My parents still laugh about that story now and it's one that usually gets rolled out over the Christmas dinner table.

That was my first ever taste of heartbreak. Even at that tender age my heart was still rather bruised and my mum said I was upset for days about the fact that Emma would probably never want to marry me now.

I still know Emma to this day; she's a dancer in Southampton. Our paths cross every now and again but thankfully I don't think she remembers a thing about the snake episode. She's still lovely but there's never been any romance between us. Maybe the snake killed our love before it had even begun? Sadly I feel like that incident kind of set the tone for the next 20 years or so when it came to my love life.

It took a little time to recover from, but I wasn't put off by that incident and so I went in search of the next young lady who would be sure to fall for my undeniable charms. Weirdly, this story also involves an animal (not in a bestiality way, dirty bastards!). The girl in question was Patricia Harris. We were both aged five when we first exchanged glances on our first day of prep school. I walked into class, probably wearing dungarees because I used to rock them, and there she was.

She had pigtails and freckles and she was American, so she seemed quite exotic. It took a while for sparks to fly, but eventually we bonded over our teacher's missing hamster. Now, I wouldn't normally advise using rodents as a way into a girl's heart, but it worked in this case.

Mrs Bonham-Smith's pet had been on the missing list for nearly a month and after a long grieving process for Bamster, everyone had given up hope of ever seeing her whiskery face again. It was widely assumed that the hamster had decided that being terrorised by children week in week out wasn't what she wanted to do with her life, so she had escaped to try and find a better one.

We never expected to see Bamster again and I imagined her trying to make her long journey to the sewers of London with some sawdust tied up in a spotted handkerchief, dreaming of the big time.

One day Patricia and I were so bored we decided to have one last search around the classroom just in case she was hiding out, and amazingly we found her snuggled up to another fugitive hamster underneath a disused sink with what looked like about a thousand baby hamsters (dirty bitch).

Patricia and I were so excited, and it seemed like such a profound shared experience at the time that I honestly thought Patricia and I were meant to be together forever (of course the Green Card would also be a massive bonus). But unfortunately, as much as she appreciated our shared interests, she was still at the stage where she found boys annoying.

I recently tried to look Patricia up on Facebook to see what she's up to these days, but I failed to find her. It may be 21 years later, she could be living anywhere in the world and look like Shrek's arse by now, but one thing I've learned about romance is that you can find it in the most unexpected places with the most unexpected people.

I have never been one to live in the moment when it comes to relationships, even though I'm spontaneous in lots of other ways. Even when I was a child I was always fast-forwarding and thinking about marriage and kids and living happily ever after within days of meeting someone. I just loved the idea of marriage, which might have had something to do with my sister's childhood fixation with *Home and Away*.

OK, so my love obsession didn't make me the coolest kid in school, because the cool ones were often rebellious and rude, but I was a sensitive dreamer. I was pretty much the anti-poon. The other kids in my school used to take the piss out of me because I was always desperate to look after both people and animals, and I could often be found in the playing fields gazing at squirrels. Once I even took home a dead squirrel I'd found so I could put it on the nature table at school the next day. Nothing says nature like a rigamortis squirrel. My parents were horrified, but I just wanted to help. The poor little thing deserved a proper grave. I also once tried to give mouth-to-mouth resuscitation to a moth. I really wish I was making that up because it sounds utterly ridiculous now I think about it, but I remember it so clearly. It happened on the same momentous day that Britney Spears released 'Baby One More Time' and whenever I hear that song it always reminds me of my attempt at giving CPR to, let's face it, a fucking ugly butterfly.

OK, so I have always been, and probably always will be, a hopeless romantic, which has been my downfall time and time again. When I was about eight I was living in a place called Abbott's Way in Southampton with my parents and Amelia. To all intents and purposes we were very happy in this fabulous house that had an amazing garden and tennis courts. My dad worked in property and my mum was a housewife. It was very much a cosy family home. Aside from my animal obsession, I was *kind of* like any other normal 8-year-old. I watched *Pete's Dragon* on repeat and had unsuccessful tennis lessons. I thought myself incredibly lucky to be living in this amazing family and I didn't really have a care in the world – my life was stable and wonderful. Or so I thought.

My parents were never that affectionate with each other when I was a child, to the point where I often used to try to sneak up on them after bedtime to see if I could catch them kissing just so I would know for sure that they loved each other.

So it shouldn't have been a surprise when, on one grey, drizzly autumn day, everything changed. Amelia and I were sat watching *Pete's Dragon* on TV when Mum and Dad walked into the sitting room. They sat down on our two pink pouffes – the height of early 90s chic – and Amelia and I knew straight away that they had something very serious to discuss with us.

I think it was Mum who took the stand first and announced in the kindest way possible that they were going to get divorced. At that age, we didn't really understand what they meant at first and it was all very confusing, until they explained that although they were still going to be friends, they would no longer be married to each other.

They had seemed so content that it made no sense to me at all. I remember sitting very still and taking it all in. I just stared at them with a blank expression while my sister cried beside me. I think I was too young to really get my head around the enormity of what they were telling us, whereas Amelia was that bit older so she knew what it meant in the long term.

They tried to help us get to grips with the fact that they were going to be living apart, but I couldn't understand why they didn't love each other anymore.

It took a long time for it to properly sink in, but once it did a small part of the fairytale had died.

I was worried that they wouldn't be happy any more, and I wondered how they could bear being apart from each other when they had shared a house, a bedroom ... everything. It seemed like a very odd thing to do, and in my eight-year-old mind I thought that maybe they would just start loving each other again and it would all be fine.

My sister and I used to watch the film *The Parent Trap* and discuss how we would use the same tactics to get our mum and dad back together. We thought if we could set up some cunning situations where they had to spend time with each other, they would fall back in love and live happily ever after. But of course that's not how things work. It's funny how a child's mind thinks.

After the initial shock and sadness wore off I was secretly slightly happy when I realised that I would now have two lots of presents every Christmas and birthday. In fact, despite the divorce initially being a huge blow, I realised that the whole thing was actually going to work in my favour in the long term.

A new, weirdly exciting phase of my life was about to begin, and with more presents and two houses, I would surely look cool enough to pull any girl now ... But while I was already mentally writing out extravagant gift lists, my sister was still distraught. In my child's brain, I saw it as the start of a new chapter, whereas she saw it as the end of one. I guess everyone deals with divorce differently, and I think the best thing parents can do is to keep the kids out of it as much as possible.

My parents said they would make sure that both of my new houses had a pond, which was another massive bonus. For some strange reason I was, and still am, obsessed with fish. I'm a Pisces, so that may have something to do with it. You may (or may not) be interested to hear that I'm a keen deep-sea fisherman and have a fishing boat moored in Hayling Island, just off Portsmouth, which I take on regular excursions around the world. See, I'm not so camp after all!

Anyway, I'm getting distracted. Let's get back to the story.

From what I remember my parents' divorce was really quite amicable. Amelia and I were kept out of all of the proceedings, and not once did we see any kind of arguments between them. I don't think there was any big drama when it came to their break-up: they had simply fallen out of love with each other.

The only thing that did upset me was the idea of my dad cross-dressing. As a child, *Mrs Doubtfire* was one of my favourite films. It must have made quite an impression on me, as I once got very upset believing that the only way Dad would be able to see Amelia and I was if he dressed up as an elderly woman like Robin Williams did in the film. I think a whole generation of divorcee Doubtfire kids genuinely believed our fathers now had to become transvestites.

As I started to get older, I refused to let my parents' divorce give me a skewed attitude to relationships. I have friends from broken families and as a result they've become really cynical about love, but I believe that just because one relationship doesn't work out it doesn't mean that they're all doomed to fail. Anyway, there was no way I was going to let my parents' divorce put me off my quest for the perfect partner.

CHAPTER 2
CIGARETTES AND ALCOHOL

As part of the divorce negotiations my sister and I were given the choice of who we wanted to live with. It was a hard decision to have to make but I was a massive mummy's boy so Amelia and I lived with Mum, moving to a housing estate called Highwood Park in Hedge End, near Southampton.

Initially Dad stayed in our family home before buying a new-build in Southampton, so he wasn't far away. We saw him at least every other weekend, and continued to do so when he later bought a new house on Hayling Island. I was excited about this new beginning, but it turned out to be a horrible time. It was around 1997 and my sister had just turned 12 when she decided that she wanted to go to boarding school. I think she wanted a bit more independence and it was also her way of trying to put our parents' divorce behind her.

When Amelia left I was alone living with Mum, and it soon became clear that she wasn't coping with the divorce as well as we'd all thought she was.

Mum seemingly became terribly thin and weighed six and a half stone, and being the only person around, it fell to me to comfort her. I hated seeing her so lonely and at the time she felt like she didn't really have any sort of social life, which must have been terribly difficult for her.

As soon as I went to bed at night she would open a bottle of Martini – which would be empty by the time I came down the next morning. She would sit in the kitchen smoking hundreds of cigarettes, and playing the same two songs over and over again. The songs were Scarlet's 'Independent Love Song' and 'Don't Cry For Me Argentina' from the *Evita* soundtrack, and even now when I hear them I am instantly transported back to those Martini days.

Even though she was obviously very low, I never regarded Mum's drinking phase as her being an alcoholic. It was more of a, 'I'm going to get drunk and forget all my troubles because that's what I need to do right now' kind of thing. *Ab Fab*, if you will. In years to come I was to know exactly how she felt. To this day Mum is my absolute rock, and we get drunk and talk about life and love and dance to 'New York, New York'. She is my favourite person on this earth.

Mum was paying for half of our school fees so she had no money at all. Any spare cash she had after she had bought the household essentials went on Martini and presents for us. She bought me a gecko called Spike from a car boot sale for being good at school, and he soon became my confidant. I felt so terrible for her, but as a 10-year-old I couldn't do an awful lot to help, except cuddle her whenever she needed me to.

I have no idea what happened money-wise when my parents went their separate ways, but I do know we were really struggling.

Dad is a wealthy man these days, but I don't know if he had money back then. He's not someone who flaunts it – he lives in a normal house and drives a normal car. Amelia and I always went to private schools, but I had no idea at the time that that was anything to do with wealth. To be honest, I just assumed everyone paid for education. A private education is all I've ever known and when I was that age I assumed everyone attended a school that resembled Hogwarts.

All of her life Mum had dreamed of becoming a radio presenter. She's blonde and glamorous and always looks immaculate so she would be amazing on TV, but radio has always been her passion and she would do anything she could to be involved in that world. Some of my most vivid memories of childhood involve me spending hours on end in radio studios in my pyjamas because Mum was working at Max FM most evenings.

The work was all voluntary and the radio station probably reached about 50 people in the Southampton area. It was the most unglamorous place you could imagine. We'd have to stay there until 11pm and I'd often fall asleep on the sofa of the studio. I remember getting very excited when Mum used to give me 20p to go and get a hot chocolate. It was the highlight of those long nights.

It got to a point when in order to earn a bit of spare cash Mum took a job delivering videos to the local video rental shop. She was paid £80 a week, but £70 of it went on babysitters for me when she was out delivering.

I remember my best friend Rupert's mum sneaking kitchen rolls and cigarettes into our house and hiding them so Mum didn't realise. She'd stumble across them and assume she'd bought them and forgotten about them. How she never caught onto it I'll never know!

Also, most of my clothes were handed down to me from Rupert, but back then he was a lot fatter than me so I spent most of the 90s in clothes that were 'you'll grow into them' huge, and often had a massive 'Gap' logo on the front. Not very chic, I'm sure you'll agree.

Rupert's parents, Joanna and Charles, later discovered that he was hiding boxes of cereal in his bedroom to eat throughout the night, which sparked the weight issue. Rupert hit puberty alarmingly early, and had he not been caught with cereal and shed the pounds he would have resembled a young, bum-fluffed version of George Michael, which is never a good look. His mum made sure he got his upper lip sugared regularly for the next two years until he learned to shave. Sugaring is basically waxing, but camper – especially when you're meant to be shaving.

There are 12 days between Rupert and I and we've been best friends ever since we were born. If it's at all possible, his love life has been more disastrous than mine. We've basically grown up bonding over masturbation stories, and a series of crap relationships. He now works as a very serious doctor and is still useless in love.

I used to spend half my life at Rupert's house when I was growing up and I always felt slightly inferior because his parents were still together and very much in love. They lived in a gorgeous house, had horses and money was never a problem. Rupert would always have the latest PlayStation games, whereas I would be a year or so behind because they always went down in price when their popularity waned. I would virtually live on his bedroom floor for weeks after the latest release. The day he was given a DVD player was momentous because they were so rare, and we were glued to his sofa for an entire summer as we made our way through a series of Jilly Cooperesque, soft-porn, 80s rom-coms that his mother favoured.

Rupert's house was stylish, always immaculate and smelt like you were walking into The White Company. It was a heady mix of fresh laundry and beautifully scented diffusers, candles and room sprays, whereas my house was more Martini and Air Wick plug-in. Mum went through a stage of putting vinegar everywhere because apparently it gets rid of the smell of smoke, but it just made everything smell very acidic and the saucers of light brown liquid looked terribly unsightly.

Joanna and Charles are the kind of parents that you dream of ultimately having as your mother- and father-in-law one day. Joanna is very glamorous and completely mad. On more than one occasion I've caught her hoovering at 7am completely naked, or walked into their bedroom to find her, again naked, frying under her personal sunbed with a cocktail.

I'll never forget the time Rupert and I decided to go though her knicker drawer for some reason, and we discovered a collection of vibrators that could rival Cheska's. I think Charles just accepts his wife's eccentric ways after 40 years of marriage.

When I was a kid all I wanted to do was go out and play with Rupert, or sit in my room pretending I was a marine biologist. I'd spend a lot of time reading the notes the Whale and Dolphin Conservation Society sent me about my adopted killer whale, Sharky.

I learned from the silent days I whiled away in my bedroom that being alone is my idea of hell. There is nothing I hate more than having to spend time in my own company – I have no one to laugh at my stupid jokes or listen to my woes. I need to bounce off other people.

Nowadays, if ever I do find myself on my own I make sure there are two bottles of red wine and 40 cigarettes to keep me company. I'll watch *Will and Grace* or *Sex and the City* because they always talk about sex and relationships, so it feels just like being with Binky and Cheska.

If you speak to anyone who went to boarding school they will always say the worst thing about it was going back on a Sunday evening after a weekend at home. Especially during winter when it was raining and cold and you'd been pulled from the comfort of your bedroom following a warming Sunday roast and a David Attenborough special.

One particular Sunday Mum and I were returning home from taking Amelia back to her boarding school listening to the radio, as we always did. Elton John had just released 'Candle in the Wind' and I remember that it was playing on the car radio while we talked. I was thinking how lucky Amelia was that she was going to be spending all week staying with her friends in her dorm in a constant sleepover. Something clicked and I turned to Mum and told her that I wanted to go to boarding school like her.

My mum later told someone that was one of the saddest days of her life, because although she really didn't want me to go, she couldn't stop me. It was my choice and my decision and I had to make my own fate in life.

I've always followed my instincts and it felt like the right place for me to be. I wish I had understood back then what my mum must have been feeling. She had been through a divorce. She was living in a new house with no money, and spending her evenings with nothing but a bottle of Martini for company. It must have felt like the final straw when her youngest child decided he wanted to leave home, aged nine.

Later that month I started to board at the same school as Amelia: West Hill Park in Titchfield, Hampshire. Because I had already been a day pupil at the school I had friends, so I felt OK about being away from home and I thought I would be fine. I took my teddy (imaginatively called Teddy) with me, as well as Whaley (I think you can probably guess what he was). Teddy has long since retired and he now sits on Mum's bed. I also took my Spice Girls *Spice* album with me, which was one of the first albums I ever had and still one of the greats. So with baggy clothes, my luxury items and a bowl haircut, I started boarding school.

My first day was like any other, but it came as quite a shock to not go home to my own bedroom when the end-of-school bell rang. Instead, I was going back to a room of 15 boys. I kept telling myself I would get used to it and I was going to have the time of my life. For the first months I found it quite scary and I remember crying a lot in the night, so I must have been terribly homesick.

The building was rumoured to be haunted and there was something called the midnight dash that new boys could do to prove their worth. You had to run through the dorms, past the headmaster's room, then through a door that took you to the back of the stage in the main hall. That area was terrifying anyway, let alone in the dead of night. The idea was that you would get all the way to the dining hall, where you would grab a knife, fork and spoon to prove you'd been there, and then you had to run back upstairs, quietly slide past Matron's office, and get back into your own dorm. If you could do that, you were really cool. I was never that cool. Instead, my friends and I took the other option and used to spend our spare time singing our favourite Disney songs in the dorm. Far less rock and roll, but I was never going to be one of the top boys who ruled the school, even when I was older.

I'm horrendously dyslexic and back then I had absolutely no passion for learning. I'm creative so I know what I want to say and how I want to say it, but it was hard for me to get things down on paper at that time. I would stare out of the window and think of things I would much rather be doing. As a result I was never top of the class, which upset me greatly as I am a total perfectionist.

I know it sounds very worthy, but to make myself feel better I started getting involved in anything to do with charity. I've always genuinely liked doing things for charity, and also it gave me a focus away from the academic side of things.

I used to win the Charity Shield every year because I was involved in every good cause going. To be completely honest, I knew that the teachers couldn't get angry if I said I was spending time raising money for the homeless when I should have been doing my homework – a foolproof plan. It wasn't that I wasn't clever and capable, because I was. I just rather liked the idea of being an actor and had absolutely no interest in academia, especially in subjects that I knew would never be of use to me, like algebra, which is complete bollocks. If you really don't understand it, move on, you'll never need it.

As I got a bit older I realised that fame wasn't just going to come knocking without me having any kind of talent. Back then, fame to me was Cilla Black and Dale Winton. It was the old legends that reigned supreme and they had worked bloody hard to get where they were.

Therefore I decided I needed to pursue a passion that might one day help me to become an actor. So I began to work enormously hard on becoming a real

Shakespearian actor. I started reading his plays and attempting to act them out when no one else was around. I dreamed about being on the stage at The Globe Theatre wearing purple tights and quoting lines from *Hamlet*. Instead I've ended up making a living out of being completely ridiculous on reality TV. Funny how things turn out!

CHAPTER 3

CANDLE IN THE WIND

I never felt outnumbered by my mum, her sister and their friends. I still saw my dad a lot so I had a strong male role model, and I also had a lot of male friends, so I think I had a good balance, and this kept me as straight as possible for as long as it could.

Ever since I can remember I've hung around with people who were seemingly more mature than me (many of my best friends are now in their 50s) and school was no different. Well, the other kids weren't in their 50s, but I was hanging around with the guys in older years so I could learn from them – especially about girls. The older boys were at the kissing/feeling up stage, which was far more exciting than our silly crushes that were clearly going nowhere. It would be years before I'd even get to glimpse my first pair of boobs.

Until then, the standard reaction amongst the boys in my year was that girls were just a bit shit – they were boring and they cried. But suddenly things had changed and they started to see girls as something other than an annoyance.

The first girl I ever properly fell for at boarding school was called Olivia. I was around nine or 10 and I remember thinking that she was incredible. She had long blonde hair and she sucked her thumb a lot so her teeth were quite goofy, which at the time I obviously thought was quite attractive. She also had a large mole above the right side of her lip, just like Cindy Crawford, who was one of my pin-ups at the time.

I was obviously very shallow back then because I quite clearly remember telling her that she could never, ever, ever cut her hair because she would no longer be pretty.

I had known her since I was born because her parents used to get drunk with my parents back in the day, but over a very short period of time she evolved from being a girl I'd run away from as fast as my lace-up Kickers would carry me to being someone I wanted to lose my snogging virginity to.

Crushes are such strange things, and more often than not, they can go horribly wrong. If I ever have kids I will tell them not to stare at someone you like, which I was guilty of. I was a fortified starer. When I was a bit older I also had a habit of drawing hearts and putting mine and a girl's name inside. Trust me, that was cool in the 90s.

Olivia was the first girl I properly snogged, but I can't remember it in much detail. I remember that we were in the living room at my mum's house during a weekend break, and I was desperate to kiss Olivia. The only problem was that Ricky was also there. He was one of my best friends at the time, so we took turns going behind the sofa to snog Olivia. Which now sounds very slutty …

I was horrified that Olivia spent more time kissing Ricky than me. He had already kissed Melanie Bell three times so he should have at least let me take the lead on this one. Heartbreak number two. I blame Ricky for tainting my first kissing experience and I'm not sure I'll ever truly be able to forgive him. I know he lives in America now, so at least he's on another continent …

I honestly couldn't tell you whether or not that first kiss was a good one, but I'm pretty damn sure it was awful. It's entirely possible I've blocked it all out in the name of self-preservation and not to harm my ever-so-fragile ego. I suspect I used the dreaded 'washing machine' technique favoured by so many, or even the infamous poker kiss, or, my favourite, the face licker. These days I pride myself on being a reasonable kisser. I've had nearly 15 years of practice, so if I was still crap I should probably retire now!

None of us really knew what we were doing back then, so we just opened our mouths, moved our tongues around a bit and hoped for the best.

I continued to spend a lot of time with Olivia and had become so smitten with her that I even tried to ride a bike without stabilisers past her house to impress her, but sadly I would often fall off my bike and look like a twat.

She really fancied this guy called Ben Ridgeway, who was by far the coolest guy at school and I envied everything he had. His father was one of the heads of Virgin Atlantic and he had beautiful older sisters. But above all, he had a centre parting, which was the epitome of cool in the mid-90s.

If you could train your hair to have a centre parting in 1995 you pretty much had girls on tap. For the best part of a year I worked on training my hair so I could look more like Ben, and convince Olivia that I was every bit as cool as him. Annoyingly, even now, in 2013, if I let my hair fall naturally it will go straight into a centre parting, making me look like a complete bell end, because I was so persistent with training it.

Olivia went through the whole of school as the popular girl, and even though I was a loser, the fact that I knew her out of school raised my coolness stake. Even though I never did get to make her my girlfriend, we became best friends and I always loved her. When we reached our mid-teens we made a pact that we would lose our virginity to each other in a caravan my mum owns in Cornwall – it's more romantic than it may sound.

We never did have sex. If only it had happened. Maybe then I would have been able to avoid the horror of what happened on that fateful day when I eventually had sex for the first time. I still shudder slightly at the thought of it. Don't worry, we'll come on to that a bit later.

Although we don't see that much of each other now, I still speak to Olivia and she occasionally comes to stay in my flat in London, and she will always sleep in my bed. I don't love her any more in that way. In fact, we help one another through all our relationship trials and tribulations. I can't imagine not having her in my life, though we never discuss how much I used to love her. I'm hoping she's forgotten about it all by now.

It's funny how some people you meet when you're young will later shape your future, whereas others you swear to stay friends with forever seem to disappear off the face of the earth once you all grow up. I still bump into people from my schooldays around Chelsea night clubs, and although I have done the drunken polite exchange of numbers and promise of a drink many times, we both know that the moment's passed and we probably no longer have anything in common. Or, to be honest, we weren't that good friends back then so why would we be any better friends now?

My tenth year was something of a disaster all round when it came to the opposite sex, as it was also the first time I ever got slapped by a girl. It was a real slap, like the ones they give out in *EastEnders*, and unfortunately it wasn't the last.

The girl in question was called Hermione Little, and looking back now she was very overdeveloped for her age. Hermione had boobs by the time she was 10 and it was all the boys could talk about. We all thought she was beautiful back then, and my sister tells me she still is. I was completely intimidated by her – everyone was – but I didn't let that put me off pathetically trying to flirt with her.

One evening before the bell for bedtime rang she was on the payphone to her mum. I was waiting in the queue behind her, feeling really homesick and desperate to talk to my own mother before bed.

Hermione was taking forever so I tried to hurry her up by banging on the door. She stormed out of the phone box, turned around and slapped me clean across the face. I was in total shock, but at the same time I rather enjoyed it. I had never seen anyone be slapped before, or been on the receiving end of one. It was the stuff of movies, like a glamorous 80s film with me in the role of the handsome phone-hassling hunk.

* * *

All other poor attempts at seduction were soon forgotten the moment I first saw Jemima Hoare (I've always pitied her name. Her teenage school years must have been a fucking pain in the ass).

Everyone else paled into insignificance. After lots of long looks, fluttering eyelashes and love notes across the classroom (all from me), I finally persuaded her to become my girlfriend. Yes, at the tender age of 10, I had found 'The One'.

I wanted everyone to know that we were 'going out' with each other and that I was in a very serious, grown-up relationship. As a result I insisted that we kissed every time we saw each other so that other people knew we were both off the market and that Hoare was mine.

I don't think she was particularly interested in me if I'm being honest. I think she mainly liked me because I was quite the rollerblader. But I also wanted her to like me for my dazzling looks and sparkling personality, neither of which I was blessed with at the time. I had half a centre-parting and half a bowl haircut, no family money, and I was weirdly obsessed with goldfish. Quite the catch, I was!

As soon as school finished I used to put my blades on and go outside the design technology block to the big open car park with my friends and we'd spend as long as we possibly could blading. Jemima always used to come and watch me and I am very happy to admit that I showed off massively to impress her.

We only 'went out' for about three weeks, but it seemed like forever back then. We broke up following an argument after I mistakenly snapped her favourite pencil. It had a troll on the top and everything so I think she felt she was left with no choice but to dump me. I was devastated, and humiliated. Heartbreak number three.

Most of the other pupils in my year had brothers and sisters who were older, so we were taking our lead from them and snogging anyone we could. I was on the rebound as a snoggingly active 10-year-old. We used to go to the local woods to run around and play kiss chase and anything else that gave us an excuse to kiss each other. I remember our teachers warning us to be careful because local yobs may be lurking in the woods. Yes, that's how posh my school was. But I was more scared about 'our' girls falling for those 'yobs' than being beaten up by them.

There was a lot of integration between the girls and boys at my school. I wasn't sporty and I wasn't wealthy like some of my dorm mates. All in all, I didn't feel like I had a lot going for me. I was also a big crier and used to get upset *a lot*. My only saving grace was that I wasn't anywhere near as bad as Paul Flynn when it came to the tears. He literally cried at everything. Even if he was late for a class he'd be sobbing in the hallway. I looked like Vin Diesel in comparison. For that reason, I will always be grateful to him.

Even though I didn't realise it at the time, I was in quite a bad place overall. I was worried about my mum, I missed my dad, I was desperate to fit in and, shit, did I have big ears! I didn't feel like I properly belonged anywhere, and on several occasions I'd hide myself away in the toilets.

Because I wasn't much of a looker and was very insecure I was an easy target for bullies. It wasn't until I was about 16 that I discovered that being funny could make me more popular. I had no idea that if you made people laugh they would like you more. It may be part of the reason why I love comedy so much now. A lot of comedians have admitted they were bullied at school and so they used comedy as a way to deal with it or escape from the bullies.

I looked so young and prepubescent that I actually wanted spots so I would seem more grown up. I'll never forget being in Boots with my sister. I was buying Clearasil to try and seem mature, and just to embarrass me in front of the woman on the cash desk Amelia shouted, 'You don't even *need* it. You don't even get spots.' My mum turned around and said, 'It's preventative, darling.' Brilliant. I had the perfect excuse to hand over my money and trot back to boarding school with my badge of hormonal honour.

Although we bickered a lot, my amazing sister kind of saved me at that school. She ran the school tuck shop, so that made me a little bit more popular than I otherwise would have been. I had an allowance of

£5 a week, which was a lot of money in those days, and I was allowed to put anything I bought from the tuck shop on the school bill. That was the dream.

If I wanted to impress a girl I would get an entire box of sweets and flash them around. Like bankers buying bottles of vodka in London night clubs, you may look like a bit of a pretentious twat, but it gets the ladies running. They may not have fancied me, but I could lure them over with a bag of Space Invaders. Or, if it was summer, an ice-pop. The ice-pop was considered the king of sweets. You couldn't get much better.

I'm probably making boarding school sound slightly dreadful, but it wasn't all that bad. I would definitely send my kids to that very school because I discovered so much about life. When you're stuck in a dorm with an eclectic mix of kids you find out so much about people. You have the cool kid, the nerdy kid, the brainy kid, the goth kid (Richard Dinan – yes, seriously). You see things from all angles and it's such a learning curve.

Amelia and I were always arguing as children. We fought like cat and dog and love-hated each other in the way siblings often do. It was probably only a couple of years ago that we properly started getting on as grown ups, and now we're like friends as well as brother and sister.

After several months of worrying non-stop about my mum, things took a massive upturn when she landed a job by complete fluke. Mum was still working for Max FM when she got scouted by the BBC. At the time, she was talking about chlamydia and sexual diseases on a midnight show listened to by about three university students, yet she managed to get spotted by a man called Chris Van Schaick. It turned out he was the head of the BBC in Hampshire, and later that week he gave her a job as a presenter on BBC Radio Solent, where she stayed for the next 12 years.

After that, everything changed. There was no more delivering videos or late nights spent at the bottom of a Martini bottle. We moved house to a lovely place in the centre of Southampton and we started a new chapter in our life.

CHAPTER 4

NO PUBES AND A SOGGY BISCUIT

My first celebrity crush, which started when I was eight, was Denise van Outen, who very slowly became my dream girl. My friend's mum worked for Channel 4 and she invited us to go along to the filming of *The Big Breakfast*. I fell in love with Denise the moment I met her. I remember her giving me a friendly wink, and I totally decided that she was the one. I grinned all the way home and I used to scour my mum's magazines for pictures of her, which I would tear out and plaster all over my bedroom walls.

By the time I was 11 my obsession had properly kicked in – probably along with my hormones. I used to sign RDA – meaning Respect Denise Always – after my name every single time I wrote it. Perhaps Ollie Locke RDA still adorns the toilet walls and classroom tables at my old school? I remember being genuinely upset when she got engaged to Jay Kay because I was convinced that she would love me if she got to know me. I almost threw a party when the engagement was called off, and it made me fall for her even harder.

Now, the awful thing is, I've since got to know her and bump into her every few months at parties around London, where we double-cheek kiss and I try not to say anything stupid. And recently, at an Elton John AIDS Foundation benefit, to my horror I was sat next to Jay Kay. I certainly did not tell him of my childhood hatred towards him for stealing my woman.

If Denise reads this book, she'll know that I was once her biggest fan. Imagine if I ever told her that I've still got the newspaper cutting from when she got engaged to Jay Kay in an old diary somewhere? Mortifying.

Denise kind of bridged the way between me being a little kid and heading, confused and bewildered, into puberty. I knew I wasn't a boy any more because I was about to start my first year of high school, but I was far from being a man. I wasn't quite sure where I slotted in.

I think puberty is one of the hardest things we go through. My top tips would be to wear deodorant and wash your face thoroughly every night. Also, don't pick spots. I did, and I've got three small scars as a result.

When I was 12 I moved schools and started going to Embley Park, which is a small boarding school based in Florence Nightingale's old family house in Romsey, Hampshire. It was the most beautiful school and I'd look out every morning and see deer on the golf course. Yes, the school had a golf course. Ridiculous, I know.

I went out with a succession of girls while I was there. I hadn't really expanded my relationship skills since Jemima Hoare, so it was very much about holding hands and imagining that you'd be together for eternity, then dumping one another by letter the next day but feeling terribly grown up while doing so.

I was now with a completely different group of people to those I'd been friends with at my last school, so it was a chance to reinvent myself a bit. I was determined I would no longer be 'Oliver the loser' with unruly hair (yes, you may be surprised to know that those silky locks once had a mind of their own). I started to buy hair gel so I could literally stick my centre parting to my forehead if it didn't behave itself, giving it absolutely no choice to move. Who's cool now, Ridgeway? I also changed my name to Ollie and stopped talking about fish quite as much as I had done previously.

I started to actually enjoy school for the first time ever. I still wasn't great academically, but I got much more involved in singing and acting. It was a brilliant way to express myself, and taking part in school productions gave me a focus. It's hard to imagine the link, but it also gave me the opportunity to fondle my first ever pair of boobs.

The boobs in question belonged to a girl called Tiffany, who was known to, ahem, put out. Hence I went for her. I was 14 by this time and we were putting on a show called *Space Queen Malajusta and the Video Kidz*. It was no *Hamlet*, but it would do for now. I had a starring role as an ageing superhero and I felt pretty awesome.

One night after the show Tiffany and I crept behind a rail of coats and started snogging. It must have been the super-hero confidence that made me slyly slide my hand under her top and inside her bra and have a grope. She certainly didn't try to stop me at any point so I was absolutely over the moon. If Twitter had been around back then I would have posted my triumph in seconds. She had really big boobs and I was thrilled to have finally felt a real one, nipple and all. It was everything I expected and more. Apart from how they actually felt; in my mind I expected them to have the weight and texture of a bag of sand, but in fact they felt more like a water balloon filled with cottage cheese.

I was quite keen to repeat the episode – and hopefully gain some more experience into the bargain – but second time around, she wasn't interested. Did I grope wrong? Who was to know? Personally, I felt I was firm but gentle. Even the girl who had a bit of a rep as a go-getter didn't want to come back for seconds! Fuck it, I still got a grope.

I shared a dorm with 12 other boys, one of whom was Alfie Allen, the actor and Lily Allen's little brother. We all had to wash in these horrible showers where you had to constantly push the button in to make the water flow, and it was one of the things I dreaded most.

I was quite a late developer, and I only had a very flimsy curtain to shield myself from the queue of burly, sniggering sixth formers waiting outside.

I was always very careful about being alert at all times when showering because a guy called Donald Yang had a habit of whipping back the curtain and revealing our scrawny hairless bodies to all of our fellow pupils. I didn't want them to know I wasn't a hairy beast underneath my clothes. When I finally got my first pube that year, for some reason it was grey. I've never quite got to the bottom of why and it worried me for weeks.

I remember a guy called Ronald Westwing-Burt being very hairy from an early age and I was so jealous. Ronald even started getting chest hair, whereas my chest only decided to sprout its first hairs when I was about 23.

My friend Dan Slowen and I used to compare our underarms on a weekly basis, looking for any sign of progress in the hair department. But nothing. I was as smooth and hairless each week as the last week, much to my despair.

Dan could kind of get away with being one of the smaller, less developed boys because he was the first person at school to have a mobile phone. At the time that was incredible because they barely existed, so he was like some kind of mobile phone-wielding god. It wasn't like some of the enormous brick ones I'd seen my dad lug around either, it was quite small and neat. I was jealous.

After lights out in the dorm, we all used to huddle around his mobile and call up the porn lines that were advertised in the back of *Loaded*, then listen to them on the loudspeaker. For some reason the women were always Scottish. Dan would try to put on a sexy older voice, but as soon as he admitted he was calling from his school dorm the ladies on the other end of the line would call a halt to things with an expression that we will never forget, 'I think you're a wee bit young for this aren't you, Danny?' leaving us with no porn material to go back to our bunk beds with.

I guess those porn lines opened the door to a world of sex that I hadn't really thought about very much before. I kind of knew what sex *was*, but I didn't know how it all worked (to be honest, I sometimes still wonder). I was so innocent, and all I really knew was that frigid was a bad word and not one that you wanted to be associated with. If anyone said you were frigid you would dispute it, even though we didn't properly understand what it meant. Of course I wasn't frigid, I had felt a boob, I would always say to myself.

Sex became something that I consciously thought about, quite a lot.

OK, I'm going to break down a barrier now. I'm going to mention the unspoken act: wanking. You can only imagine how much secretive masturbation went on in the dorms – even though the likelihood was that no one was doing it properly.

We had no choice but to do it in the dorm or in the toilets, but even in these public places we could always find a way. I've heard all of the stories about boys' private schools where apparently everyone lines up in a row and has a wank, and something to do with a soggy biscuit, but that certainly didn't happen at any of the schools I was at. When you're young you're so insecure about the size of your penis that I can't imagine anyone would want to get theirs out in front of their peers. Unless, of course, you were particularly blessed in the downstairs area, in which case you would probably choose to walk around naked most of the time. As far as I was concerned it was all very much done under the covers – and under the cover of darkness.

Wanking certainly wasn't a subject that was discussed at school. I am still very grateful to this day that I was never caught with my hands down my pants. I think that would have set me back several years, and I was far from advanced to start with. It's entirely possible I'd still be a virgin now had that happened. Can you imagine?

CHAPTER 5

VALENTINE'S DAY DISASTERS

Aged 14 and still high on my first breast-groping experience, I decided that I wanted a proper girl-friend. Not the sort of hand-holding, occasional kissing type I'd had before, but a full-blown, boob-groping, bike-shed kind of one. I really fancied a girl called Evelyn Beanie, but she wasn't at all interested in me. Outrageous, I know, but I still wasn't exactly what you'd call 'a catch', and I was very inexperienced in matters of the heart. I just wanked a lot.

I never used to get any Valentine's cards and every time that 'special day' rolled around it was like a form of torture because everyone used to boast about how many cards they'd received and my granny's handwriting was always distinguishable. I was the person who would organise for the other boys to send roses and cards to girls via the school. I was the cupid and the one the teachers selected to organise everything. You could send a rose to someone you liked and add it on to your school bill so your parents ended up paying for it at the end of the year, but I always sent them to the really popular girls and never received any myself. Tragic.

I think the bottom line is that I was a loser. I didn't help myself either, for when the opportunity came to be in charge of the headmaster's fish tank I jumped at it, granting me the nickname 'Fishy'. While other people were busy groping the go-getter Tiffany, Fishy here was busy making sure the pH levels of the water in the tank were accurate. I know I've said I love all things to do with marine life, but I think this was taking it a bit far, even for me.

The squash courts were the place to go if you wanted to get down and dirty with someone. There were always stories about girls being felt up in the viewing gallery. It was legendary. I think every school has such a spot. There was one girl – who shall remain nameless – who had a real reputation for getting groped by virtually every single guy in school. She made Tiffany the go-getter look like a right prude. Apart from me, I might add; I was probably busy feeding the fish.

Looking back, I thank God that I didn't end up with my hand down anyone's pants because I wouldn't have had a clue what I was doing. It would be years before I had any understanding of the female form.

I remember learning about the, I guess you could say, technical side of sex while sitting in a science lab, playing with the gas taps to distract myself from the horror that was unfolding in front of me. Some poor teacher was made to stand facing a classroom of 14-year-olds and slide a condom over a banana as the entire room looked on in mortified fascination. It was about breeding, not pleasure, it seemed they were saying. I guess they were trying to make it sound as unsexy as possible so we wouldn't all go home and do it, underage. I should have been so bloody lucky!

I honestly think that when it comes to sex education, rather than just telling people how to avoid getting pregnant or and the ins and outs of things, as it were, they should tell teenagers *how* to actually do it. There is nothing in place to help you avoid the humiliation of being absolutely shit when you do finally manage to convince a girl to get off with you.

I remember having one absolutely awful lesson where we were shown a silky piece of material and told that we should use it, should we ever wish to perform oral sex on a girl, to prevent STDs. It was like a condom for oral sex and it was the most revolting thing I've ever seen. No one said we didn't *have* to use it.

In short, sex education taught me nothing about sex. It just left me confused and rather amused that our teacher, Mrs Oddy, had said the words 'scrotum' and 'climax' all in the same lesson. It was better than maths with Mrs Dilloway, though, I guess.

Thankfully, Rupert and I soon discovered a place where we could learn what we really needed to at that point in our lives. That place was jackinworld. com.

Jackinworld.com was a website that basically taught you how to masturbate in hundreds of different ways. Nobody at school had laptops back then, so Rupert and I used to have to wait until we had access to a computer in his dad's secretary's office and swiftly look up as much porn as possible.

We also managed to get hold of our very own porn mag. At the time they were hard to lay your hands on and they cost a fortune. Luckily we found out that Donald Yang (of the shower-curtain expose fame) was something of a porn dealer. I may have had to miss out on dishing out sweets to girls after spending a small fortune on a magazine which only featured older, hairy Chinese women, but it was such a great source of knowledge that it was worth every penny. The only problem was that Rupert ruined the one and only porn mag we had by telling me that the main centrefold could be my Chinese sister. I could never look at Cum Soong in the same light again.

We discovered porn not long after the Millennium. Yes, the anniversary to mark 2000 years since Christ's birth coincided with my discovery of pornography. At the time Nestlé had brought out a time capsule of chocolate to celebrate. The idea was that after getting a well-deserved sugar high by eating all of the chocolate in one go, you could then put interesting, timely things like photographs, love letters and four-leaf clovers inside the capsule. You were then meant to seal it up and bury it so it could be discovered by people in years to come.

Instead, I used mine as a makeshift sex capsule in which I could keep my porn without it being discovered. I've got it to this day, and it's still got the same magazine in it. It also contains the condom wrapper from the first time I ever had sex. I really should throw it all away at some point.

It seems incredible that nowadays porn is the most looked at thing on the internet, just ahead of Justin Bieber. I'm not sure what that says about today's society. I guess porn has always been big business, but now it's much more readily available. Back then we had to take it where we could get it; we'd read the *Kama Sutra*, but actually my first pornographic experience was my mum's illustrated copy of *The New Joy of Sex*.

One day I got an excited call from Rupert to say that he'd somehow managed to stream a porn film through his dad's computer and onto a VHS. He asked his dad's secretary to post a copy to me at school, telling her it was a nature documentary. Which it was. Of sorts. I suppose it did include beavers …

When it arrived it had 'The Blue Planet' written on the side. The perfect disguise. If ever I went home I took it with me to lessen the risk of any of the teachers discovering its true content, and I kept it in my bedroom along with my other films. Completely safe. Or so I thought.

One day I came home to find that my mum was ill in bed with terrible flu. She was bored so she'd gone into my room to borrow something to watch. She had nearly finished watching one of my movies, and lined up for her viewing pleasure was the 'Blue Planet' video. I have never panicked as much in my life. I had to make up some ridiculous excuse and whip it away before she had a chance to insert the tape into the machine and reveal its true contents. I still cringe now when I think about what would have happened had she chosen to watch that first instead of the other film. It doesn't bear thinking about.

We were allowed to have posters up at school, but nothing in any way rude. I had pictures of Naomi Campbell and Cindy Crawford that my cousin had given me when he'd left Winchester College. I was over Denise van Outen by then (sorry, Denise!) so supermodels became my crush of choice.

Around this time, I especially liked older women. Not necessarily in a Harry Styles way, but I adored the fact that girls taught me about life in a way that the football-obsessed boys in my year couldn't.

There was an older woman I fancied around this time, but she was actually someone I knew rather than just a model I had a poster of.

When I used to go and visit my dad in Hayling Island, I would demand he take me to the island's best fish restaurant, called The Mariner's. A girl called Nina worked as a waitress, and she was absolutely incredible. She must have been about 18 and was just amazing.

I fancied her so much that she bizarrely became the blueprint for any girl I found attractive thereafter. She was quite short and slim, with long dark hair and a big smile. She reminded me of Rhona Mitra, the actress who once played Lara Croft. I assume she used to serve me my dinner thinking I was a sweet 14-year-old, but I was actually having very improper thoughts about her while surfing the web on jackinworld.com. I once again thought she was the woman I was going to spend the rest of my life with, and she obviously had no idea that I fancied her. I would be devastated if she wasn't working when I'd inevitably drag my dad to the restaurant on one of my visits.

She was probably one of the first girls I ever seriously tried to flirt with, but instead of sweeping her off her feet I just blushed a lot, said the wrong thing, ordered *moules marinières* and tried to impress her with my weird fish knowledge. It was very awkward. She now works in a shipping yard near Portsmouth, and every now and then when I go and see my father

I bump into her mother. The last time I saw her she told me that Nina had recently got engaged to a very wealthy man. Great, so now I'm at an age where I can date older women I've missed the boat, if you'll pardon the awful pun.

I had access to quite a lot of older women around this time, and I developed crushes on quite a few. Bizarrely, I mainly remember Joanna Lumley being the object of my desire. I was still pursuing my dream of becoming an actor by doing some work as an extra on TV shows and films, so through this I met a lot of glamorous older actresses. For some reason, even though I was somewhat shy around girls of my age, I was confident with older women. I genuinely thought I had a chance. If I had met Joanna Lumley I would have tried to win her over.

Back in the real world, I started hanging out with a girl called Hazel, who I met through my school choir. She was 17 and, despite the age difference, I really fancied her. She and her friends used to let me hang around with them – they were very grown up and would talk about how their boyfriends had annoyed them by not calling or acting like dicks. I learned a lot from their more experienced insight into love, listening to everything they said and storing it for my later years, when I was certain it would all come in very useful.

I didn't have any jobs growing up like most teenagers do, apart from a three-week stint cleaning arcade machines at Hayling Island funfair. I was at boarding school all week and I didn't finish until 2pm on a Saturday, then from 3pm until 7pm I was at Stagecoach drama school.

My mum had this obsession with community church so we'd go there every Sunday. I liked the idea of religion, but I think it's something everyone should make up their own mind about. I thought it was great fun and I loved the fact that they sang and played guitars, and although it's maybe distasteful to say it, some of the church girls were seriously hot.

At one point I got so into church that I used to go and sing and dance around each week like I was in some kind of gospel choir in Texas. I loved it. I'd top it off with a roast dinner at home with my mum and sister, before returning to school to start the week over again.

My Saturday afternoon drama school was also a good way of meeting girls. I was used to quite posh girls, but the girls at drama school were totally different and more fun. They wore make-up and said 'fuck'. It was a whole new girl world to me and I loved it. I intrigued them because they thought I was very posh. They always asked me about boarding school and I think they thought I lived in a castle.

There weren't many boys in my classes because guys of that age didn't really do drama, so I got a lot of female attention. There was a girl called Sarah I really liked, and I also really fancied the principal's daughter, Gabby (not *that* Gabby before you get ahead of yourself). She didn't often do the classes but I used to text her a lot. Usually messages like, 'I can't text any more because I've got no credit'. My dazzling way with words shone through at a young age; clearly, showing that you can't afford credit is not an aphrodisiac. Gabby was a bit gothy and I thought that was very cool because she wore Green Day hoodies. God knows what Green Day was, but it looked great.

CHAPTER 6

CONER BONER AND THE PHOTO OF DOOM

As I got older, my relationships with girls turned from fascination and masturbation to an appreciation of the actual friendship you can have with them. We were all hanging around together as a big group, guys and girls together. Every one of us was transitioning into adulthood – pubes were growing, spots were shining, and we'd started to drink and smoke as an outward sign that we were very old. So much so that, at the age of 16, I actually shunned cigarettes for Café Crèmes, which are like small cigars. I hated the taste of cigars but I thought they looked awesome. In my mind, I looked like a Second World War soldier – and a seriously cool one too.

Dating was a fun game back then, and boarding school had never been more enjoyable. My search for my first proper girlfriend had lasted for a year with little – or no – success until I met Joan Lightening when I was around 15 years old. She may sound 75, but I promise she was my age, and hot. She was a tall and very beautiful redhead with a big smile. She was also very funny. After several months of dating, which consisted mainly of hand-holding, trips to the cinema and snogging like a washing machine, I sent her a letter to try to woo her into taking things to the next level. In today's world of email, text, Facebook, Twitter and BBM, that sounds very old-school and I suppose almost romantic, which it would have been, only I didn't write the letter myself. I didn't have a clue what to say so I asked an older and wiser prefect called Simon to pen it for me to increase my chances.

It said, 'I think it's about time we made our relationship more intimate.' To be honest, I had no idea what the word 'intimate' meant. I thought it was some grand romantic term, and I basically trusted Simon to write something sonnet-esque that would enable me to get some action. But rather than get me action, it got me in a lot of shit with Miss Blackwell, the head of boarding.

The letter was found by a cleaner, who then passed it on to Miss Blackwell who, to put it mildly, was less than impressed. Of course when she read it, it sounded as if we were planning to have sex on school grounds, and there were few things worse than that. Joan was in the year below me as well, so she was probably only about 14. It was horrific and marked the end of that short relationship.

I don't think I've ever cried as much as when I got summoned to the headmaster's office to explain myself. I was in so much trouble and convinced I was going to get kicked out of school. In the end my mother had to come and explain that not only was I obviously incapable of being intimate with anyone, but I obviously had no idea what the word meant.

When I was getting towards the end of my days at Embley I had finally started to grow hair down there. It's amazing to think how a few hairs can carry so much meaning, but they do. Those downy tufts of dark hair populating my nether regions and under-arms were a tangible expression of my transition from boy to man. On top of those luscious locks of Ollie Locke pubes, I was getting pretty happy with the size of my ever-growing willy. Now, you may feel that I'm going off on one here, but bear with me. The previous Christmas I had been given a camera phone and it was my pride and joy. So, one day I did what every man does but won't admit to: I took a picture of my semi-flaccid willy. Without going into too much detail, I made sure it looked as big as possible, and then I left the photo out to be found by the other boys so they would be impressed.

Needless to say they did find it, but the camera phones of 2003 weren't great, and angles and shapes came out slightly distorted. I hadn't noticed when I took it, but the photo gave the impression that my manhood, my pride and joy, was cone shaped. From that day on I was nicknamed 'Coner Boner', and it has stuck to this very day. Oliver 'Coner Boner' Locke. RDA. Thank God Fishy was dropped!

We were always up to stupid things in our dorm, and one thing we loved doing was getting glow sticks and having pretend raves. One fireworks night we discovered that if you cut the tops off the glow sticks and whip the liquid everywhere, when you turn out the lights it looks like a planetarium. But when you turn the lights back on there is no sign of the liquid. Perfect for watchful prefects on duty.

I took my art GCSE very seriously and decided that it would be an amazing idea to take a series of pictures of me with bits of my naked body covered in the amazing glow paint. As you can see, my penchant for nudity began a while ago. All you would see were the highlighted parts and nothing rude, so it didn't seem too risqué.

I got my friend Slowen to take the photos in our room, and I stood there totally naked apart from some strategically placed glow paint. Digital cameras weren't really around then, so Dan took the photos on a disposable camera, which I then planned to take to the local town to get developed the next day.

We filled the entire camera, and when we finished we both realised to our horror that Dan had used the flash for the entire thing, so instead of picking up the glowing areas, the photos would show a fully naked me, in poses which made me look slightly arty.

Even worse, I put the camera on his bedside table that night and totally forgot about it. When I then went to find it a few days later, it had disappeared. To this day I don't know what happened to it, so somewhere out there is a camera of a 16-year-old me in various naked poses. If found, please return it. Thanks.

I was totally mortified but I managed to forget my sorrow when my godbrothers Jack and Tom invited me to go to Vale do Lobo in Portugal for my first ever lads' holiday. It was a typical public school place to visit, and when we arrived everyone had big blond hair, wore their collars up and had double-barrelled surnames. They all started conversations with the questions 'What school do you go to?' and 'What do your parents do?' It was like having 10,000 mini *Made in Chelsea* characters, but with real tans, and slightly less hairy.

On one night when we went out for a drink I was instantly drawn to this unbelievable-looking girl standing at the bar, who I later found out was called Hattie Clarke.

Hattie was beyond cool. She was blonde, slim and was obviously the Queen of Vale do, even though she was only about 16. I had never seen anyone cooler or more beautiful than her.

She had trouble written all over her as she stood there smoking and doing shots, surrounded by admirers. Even from a distance I could tell that she was a proper mean girl, but so much fun. I knew I had to get close to her.

I was on holiday for two weeks and for the first week all I did was look at her, smile like an idiot and bump past her on the dancefloor in the hope she would notice me, take me onto the beach and grope me. In the second week, after a few vodkas, I plucked up the courage to talk to her.

The boys and I used to go to that same bar pretty much every night. One evening I went down there wearing combat trousers and a shirt that was too big for me, because that was the fashion at the time (or so I thought). My hair was extra-spiky and all in all, it wasn't a cool look. So with Dutch courage in the form of a couple of cocktails, I walked up to her and offered to buy her a drink. She asked for a Squashed Frog, fuck knows what that was, but I confidently ordered one as if I'd ordered hundreds before.

We bonded instantly. I knew she would fall in love with me.

We danced the Portuguese night away and for a whole week we were inseparable. She kept on telling me how cute I was, which I thought was the first step to getting into her pants. Sadly not. But being her friend was such a big deal for me that I persuaded myself something would happen between us back in England.

I went back to school after summer clutching all of my photos from the holiday. I was so proud of them that I displayed them on my dorm wall (Facebook didn't exist back then). But I had no way of keeping in touch with Hattie so our friendship fizzled out and life, as it always does, moved on. Although little did I know that wasn't the last I would see of her ...

I bounced back from Hattie pretty quickly, and continued on my quest for love and, to be honest, at that point, sex. I was 16 and by then pretty much everyone was doing it. If I didn't lose it soon, I'd be put in the same category as smelly David Woodwood-Brown, or spotty Freddy Neilson. Much to my disappointment, my subsequent encounters were all very innocent. That is, until I met a girl called Candy. Now Candy is quite obviously a fake name, but this story needs a pseudonym. She was one of my sister's bigger-breasted friends, which at that time was incredibly exciting. The boobs I first fondled were good, but by no means Candy standard.

My sister and I had travelled down to spend a weekend with my dad, and my sister had brought Candy along for the weekend. Somehow we ended up snogging. I can't remember the exact events that led up to that kiss but it was preceded by an evening at Hayling Island's premiere Indian restaurant 'The Gandhi', followed by a game of truth or dare with a very old bottle of ouzo.

Candy was 18 and half Australian, so she seemed so grown up, exotic and way out of my league. By this time I really was ready to get intimate and I now knew full well what that word meant. I was desperate for Candy to be the girl to show me the way.

My sister's bedroom at my dad's house was very small so Candy ended up coming and staying in my room, much to my delight. My dad had no idea so we had to be very quiet about it all.

We ended up fumbling around on the floor, and I got to experience my second proper boob feel. It was amazing! Even better than the first time. Not only that, but I plucked up the courage to slide my hand down her knickers. It was by far the most exciting thing that had ever happened to me. I had recently flown Concorde to New York, but nothing compared to this. I was ecstatic, though I had absolutely no idea what I was doing. I wasn't even sure that I was in the right hole. She then made the move that would change the rest of my adult life forever, as for the first time in my life, a girl touched my willy. I really had expected it to go off then, and I wish it had as she clearly hadn't got any tips from jackinworld.com. Her technique was one you would use to wring out a wet towel, while stretching it out for good measure. It was the most painful gift fate had ever given me.

I had to think fast on my feet for what to do. I could either a) claim to not be able to ejaculate, b) make a noise and run to the bathroom, or c), which at the time seemed the most logical, pretend I'd cum by spitting on her boobs and rubbing it before she realised it wasn't sperm. I honestly wish that I could say that I was lying, but I am afraid option c was very much put into action. I had no choice (other than the two above) – it was total agony. She used a completely different technique to the one I used, which kind of involved me rubbing myself with two hands as if I was trying to create a fire in the middle of a forest (I have no idea why).

My sister was furious about me getting together with Candy. In her eyes, I was still her little brother so she hated the idea of me fondling her best friend. I, however, was so excited to get back to school to tell everyone about my first proper sexual experience, with an older woman, no less.

Candy and I texted a few times after that night but nothing ever came of it, which was just as well as the Snow Ball was coming up, which was a big event in all the local public school teen's calendars.

The Snow Ball was basically a huge party held once a year that attracted all the students from boarding schools around Hampshire and Wiltshire. I would go to Moss Bros and hire a dinner jacket, stock up on cigarettes and snog as many people as possible. Nothing could go wrong. I think I managed about 15 or 16 that year, but a guy called Scott managed around 60. I was in awe of him that night; I still am.

My friends and I started going to a lot of parties, but no one particularly fancied us, I don't think. One time, we went to a friend's party. I was kissing a girl called Rosie, and for some reason she kept biting my lip. She probably intended it to be quite sexy but instead it was really painful! I ran away from her in the end because my lips were so sore, but later on in the evening my friend Josh decided to try his luck with her. I warned him about the biting, but one thing led to another and he stupidly allowed her to give him a blowjob. The next thing he knew she cut his willy open – he even had to make a little turban out of toilet roll to stop the bleeding. After that she was blacklisted within our group and everyone steered well clear of her. She was bloody dangerous.

The following week was our annual lads' ski trip. It was actually the first and only ski trip we would ever go on, but at that point we were certain that we would make it an annual thing. I was convinced that we were going to get some serious action while we were there. We were all staying in chalets and it ended up being like a posh version of *The Inbetweeners*. I'm a good skier so in my eyes I thought I would obviously come across as an alpine Gerard Butler on skis to all the girls, but the reality was we were wearing some sort of vagina-repellent aftershave. The girls all kept their distance and didn't seem to like us shouting romantic gestures from the ski lift as they passed below.

I certainly hadn't blossomed in any way at this point, and I didn't know about looking after myself so it was no wonder I wasn't at the top of every girl's kiss-list. I had bum fluff, which at the time I called my beard, and I wouldn't dream of shaving it off. It had taken 17 years to grow so I walked around like some sort of lizard.

It was around this time that I first started to grow my head hair in order to look like a model called Travis, who was the face of Calvin Klein for years. Then I tried blond highlights in order to emulate Charlie Simpson from Busted, who back in my late teens was the coolest man and owner of the best eyebrows, before I settled on trying to morph into 'Smith' Jerrod from *Sex and the City*. I'm sure I thought that if I had similar hair I would magically develop amazing muscles, have women hanging on my every word and a lucrative contract to advertise expensive vodka.

Throughout our entire childhood Rupert and I would compare notes on girls, and there was always an air of competition simmering under the surface about who would lose their virginity first. We were both fairly innocent, even at 16, and desperate to be the first to have sex. Most of our friends had already started, and we were beginning to look (even more) uncool.

Rupert had been single for a while when he was introduced to a girl called Grace. She was incredible; they became inseparable and things soon got serious between them, much to my secret annoyance.

As a result Rupert stopped looking at jackinworld. com and started looking at sex websites just in case by some miracle she decided that she wanted to go all the way with him. He needed to know what to do in case the opportunity should ever, ahem, arise.

A few months later they did sleep together and although I was pleased for them, I was slightly gutted that he was steaming ahead of me in the sex stakes. Operation 'Get Laid' was becoming disastrous. As research for this book, Rupert kindly called up Grace to ask her some questions about how he performed the first time they had sex, but awfully she was at her grandmother's funeral at the time. That could only happen to Rupert. He's still wondering, by the way, Grace, so do let us know.

Rupert and Grace dated for about two years in total, and although their relationship made me a bit envious, it also opened up a whole new world of opportunities for me because she would bring her friends along with her when we went out.

Grace took a group of us to a party hosted by one of her friends and a girl there, Lucie, started to show some real interest in me. Being completely honest, I thought she was a little bit chavvy, but of course there was a chance that she could also be the answer to my virginity prayers.

I got quite drunk and decided it was the perfect time to smoke weed for the first time in my life. Needless to say, I got absolutely fucked. Weed is an awful drug, especially uncool when your eyes look like a bloodshot Halloween mask and you get the munchies so you're trying to snog someone with Pickled Onion Monster Munch around your face.

Lucie took me upstairs to the landing, where we lay on the floor, and with no warning whatsoever she slid herself down my body as if she was about to give me a blowjob. I have never been so scared in my entire life. I ended up telling her I hated them, as if I'd done it loads of times before. I'd been waiting so long for this moment, but when the elusive blowjob was on the cards, I wouldn't let her. Was I frigid? Were the kids at school right?

For some reason we then ended up going into her bathroom, where we slid into the empty bath (God knows why), where all my Christmases came at once – we proceeded to try and have real sex. All those years of desperate longing had built up to this and I was so excited about finally becoming a fully-fledged, sexual being, with the added benefit of it being in such circumstances that would provide me with a great story to tell all of my friends.

In my mind it was inevitable that as soon as I got the chance to actually do it, I was going to discover that sex was something I was very good at. I seemed to have some adequate rhythm on the dancefloor, so why not in the bedroom? I was sure that it would prove to be a real hidden talent.

But … I couldn't get it up. The one time in my life when I needed him the most, he decides he's gonna chill out. I would usually get a boner everywhere; the bus, the train, a mobile phone vibrating. Even my electric toothbrush would cause a real erectile commotion. But with a naked girl in front of me, who was obviously up for it, he decides, fuck it, I'll have a nap. I was worried that she would go downstairs and tell my friends that not only could I not get a boner, but at aged 16 I didn't have the biggest willy. That would have been a disaster, but as a female equivalent of a gentleman, she did nothing.

I acted as chilled as possible, but inside I was dying. I wonder what she's doing now.

Looking back I am so bloody relieved that I didn't lose my virginity that night. It would have been an awful virginity story to have to tell. Nearly as bad as my actual one … but we'll have to wait at least a year for that.

CHAPTER 7

NOT-SO-SWEET SIXTEEN

———

I was 16 and a virgin with apparent erectile dysfunction issues. Needless to say I was a complete loser. It seemed as though everyone else in the world apart from me was now having sex. I was gutted.

There were three schools in my area – mine, Embley, a girls' school called The Atherley, and Stanbridge Earls, where my friend Pugsley's dad was headmaster. This meant we had access to things like quad bikes, the swimming pool and all the land at Stanbridge Earl's every week. Every month when his parents were away, Pugsley used to have epic house parties, which provided amazing opportunities to meet girls. He once threw a Halloween party for which I decided to prepare myself by buying a £2.99 lads' mag with the coverline: 'How to get a woman into bed'. In the accompanying piece it said that women liked it when men have a hairless pubic region as it makes your willy look bigger. I was amazed. I had been so worried about growing pubes, I never even considered what women might like. I got straight in the shower, found Mum's Venus razor, and went to town. I walked into that party like a new man.

I had decided to dress as Superman, but for some reason I wore a red PVC thong, which was stuffed with a cricket box to protect my modesty. It was February, and still rather chilly. I thought I looked amazing. My hair had a new spiky style and I felt awesome.

There was a girl at the party who had apparently seen my photo and, despite the floppy hair with centre parting and complete lack of dress sense, liked what she saw. When we met I immediately started whipping out my 16-year-old flirting techniques, which mainly involved dancing awkwardly to Kelly Rowland songs and participating in a WKD drinking competition, but it worked like a charm.

She made it very clear that she wanted to do more than kiss, so after some dancefloor snogging and three Bacardi Breezers I suggested that we go up to one of the bedrooms. I knew that Pugsley's brother Logan was away at university so his room was free.

We then proceeded to undress each other as if we were appearing in an episode of *Hollyoaks*. We were down to our underwear when she started to get *very* frisky. I wasn't really expecting it and dreaded her going anywhere near my willy. You see, my prior confidence at my newly shaved pubic region had quickly evaporated when, after a few Bacardi Breezers, I told Rupert what I'd done. He nearly had a seizure laughing and said that any girl would be freaked out by my lack of hair as it would just look as though I hadn't grown it yet. So I didn't really want her thinking that I didn't have pubes.

Unsurprisingly, given my complete failure in the women department, I had never before performed oral sex on a girl, but I decided that it would be the best way to distract her from my downstairs area. I'd never really thought about what you did once you were down there and I'd never actually seen a vagina up close apart from in my early teen porn mags. So, I whipped out my secret weapon, the essential latex oral sex, STI preventer: my eight-inch by eight-inch piece of flat latex, which I unwrapped and displayed like a delicate napkin. So with protection in front of me, I spent about 20 minutes licking her pubes. Not living up to her name, Mona, I could tell she was lying there thinking 'well, this is awkward' and pretending to enjoy it. She didn't say a word, but in retrospect, I wonder if she actually knew whether I was doing it wrong or if it was her first time too. God, it's so awful when I look back on it. It really was a disaster.

As we went so far together that night, I became convinced that I would definitely have sex very,

very soon. I felt like I was so close to becoming a man and that was the final piece of the puzzle. Even if I did still look about 12, which was a problem compounded by the fact that my best friend, Slowen, who had always been the smallest in our friendship group, had suddenly started to blossom. He had been put on a course of steroids to help his growth and when they kicked in he shot up and ended up having the most incredible body you've ever seen in your life. He was totally ripped, good-looking and also funny, so he started to become a real hit with the ladies. Meanwhile I still had no game whatsoever. Being yourself just wasn't the thing to do. It was about making yourself seem really aloof and unattainable, but I was just too eager to please.

When I wasn't dressing up as Superman my style was generally awful. It's hard to imagine, I know. I wore big Fubu skater jeans and trainers. My inspiration came from Rupert's sister, who was a real skater girl and always looked really 'street' and cool. Rupert and I both tried to steal her style. I didn't have a skateboard, but I had my Bauer rollerblades, which I thought made me look very credible and almost gave me permission to dress the way I did. How wrong I was.

I spent most of my late teens going on holidays to Rock in Cornwall. When Mum had no money she wanted to make sure that my sister and I still had holidays with her, so when I was 12 she ended up borrowing a run-down campervan from a friend, which we took to Rock, much to mine and Amelia's embarrassment.

We ended up falling totally in love with the place and that Christmas Granny bought us our own caravan in Polzeath. Now before you all imagine me as even more of a loser, they are awesome, and I stand by that.

To many people a caravan is their idea of hell. But I don't mind admitting that I love a good caravan and they have resulted in some of the best memories of the last 10 years. Polzeath is a lovely family holiday spot with great restaurants and beautiful beaches. It wasn't particularly well known when we first started going there, but one summer Princes William and Harry were photographed surfing on Polzeath beach, and this automatically made it the coolest place for anyone from public school to go to. For once, and it's still pretty cool, I was ahead of the game.

Even now Cornwall is very important to me. It's not just a place I go to when everything is going well, but also when everything goes wrong. There have been times when I've had break-ups and low points and I've driven myself down there in the middle of the night so I can be somewhere completely alone. It's so beautiful and I can sit and think and try to deal with what's going on in my life. Usually it's something to do with a relationship.

Port Isaac is just down the road, which is where the TV show *Doc Martin* is filmed. It's completely idyllic. Port Quin, now that's the place I go to when I'm *really* upset. It's my own little secret spot. There's a seat there that has 'OL' and 'PH' carved into it – mine and Pugsley's initials – which we did when we were 14. I love going there to get inspiration. It's one of the only places where I don't mind being alone. It's a little cove in the middle of nowhere and very few people know about it.

The only problem with the caravan was the portable loo. No one wanted to empty the caravan loo at the end of the week, so trips to the freezing-cold shower block were the only way forward.

However, the legend of the Beast of Bodmin, which is about a giant wild creature akin to Bigfoot that lives on the moor, was always at the back of our minds. I don't mind admitting that I was seriously worried that it did actually exist, and that I would be hunted down by it. Needing a wee at 2am and going to the loo on your own is a no go. So Pugsley and I would often resort to weeing into a plastic bottle, which by the end of the holiday became a game of who could fill it up the most. Pugsley usually won; damn his northern bladder.

If anyone on the site annoyed Pugsley and me we used to sneak out in the middle of the night after a few bottles of wine and put bread on the top of their caravan roof so that in the morning they would be woken up by the sound of hundreds of seagulls scratching at the roof. At the very least we'd hope it would cut short their lie-in, even better if they thought the beast was attacking them.

By the time I was 16 I had some friends who could drive, so we used to head off to the caravan for the weekend on our own. We decided to spend the summer after our GCSE exams hanging out on the beach drinking a rather lethal mix of Rattler cider and beer, and trying to feel up girls. It was one of the best times of my life.

To celebrate the end of exams, we decided to go to what was probably the only club there. I still looked quite young for my age, so I knew I had very little chance of getting in – even with the fake ID I had ordered from an advert I found in the back of *Loaded* magazine.

I came up with this ingenious idea of sticking some of my pubes to my chest using Pritt Stick to make me look older than I was. The sun was setting over Cornwall and I went to the caravan drawer and found some old Scrabble pieces, the ever-present pack of condoms, and a Pritt Stick. I originally planned to use some of my head hair, so I took the kitchen scissors and snipped it off, but it didn't look right: it was too straight. So I went into the bathroom, cut off 40 per cent of my pubes, which had just grown back, and tried to stick them onto my chest.

My sister knew exactly what I was doing and she found it hilarious, but I was the one with the smile on my face later than night. I swear to God, it worked.

With my summer tan, long hair and wispy beard, I looked like a Greek god. Well, a Greek god with Pritt-Stick chest pubes. I felt so smooth – it was a major triumph.

With the summer sadly coming to an end it was time to go back to school. I decided to move schools to do my sixth form years. I felt like I'd grown out of Embley Park, so Mum and I looked around for other places. Bizarrely, I chose a Quaker school called Sibford in Banbury, Oxfordshire.

When I went for the initial interview the headmaster told me that they couldn't let me in because I had failed GCSE maths, and they urged me to re-take it. I replied in no uncertain terms that I would rather eat my own scrotum than re-take that ghastly exam and I asked them to take me even without the proper qualification. I must have been pretty convincing because they agreed to let me in.

I didn't know anyone else when I enrolled at Sibford because all of my friends stayed on at Embley Park. It was quite hard leaving them but we stayed in touch via phone and, although it seems very old-fashioned now, we sent each other letters.

I knew I wasn't the coolest kid by any stretch of the imagination, but as soon as I started there something shifted and suddenly for the first time I seemed to be popular. I decided to mark this transition, this fresh start, by dyeing my hair blond. As you do.

I wanted to look like Charlie from Busted, but I ended up looking more like an early Gary Cockerill, one of Katie Price's glam squad. Needless to say, it wasn't a strong look, but my fellow pupils were quite country bumpkin-ish, and I am not sure they had ever seen hair dye since *Top of the Pops* was decommissioned. Also, I was different and much more streetwise. I had grown up on the mean streets of Southampton. Well, sort of. I also pretended to be something of an actor, which I think some of my fellow students considered quite cool.

I was still desperate for a girlfriend, for that elusive serious relationship which, despite years of persistent searching still hadn't materialised. Being at a new school surely afforded me the chance to meet someone?

On the very first day when I walked into the lunch hall there was a girl sitting alone who stood out from all the rest.

She was called Tilly – and she was just incredible. She was very skinny, with long brown hair, and wore the shortest skirts you can imagine. She was like Nina the barmaid, but sluttier. And, more importantly, she was my age.

I had befriended Ed, the head of sports, and he introduced me to Tilly over a sandwich. In my usual subtle style and with absolutely nothing to lose, I asked her if she had a boyfriend. She smiled coyly and said no. After having a small celebration in my head (and pants) I decided that one day soon I would make her my real girlfriend.

I later found out through various people she had been lying and that she had a long-term boyfriend. This confused me. Why would she say she was single if she wasn't? It was too late, I had already fallen for her. And from that initial meeting she went on to play a huge part in my life, as for the next two years Tilly and I were completely inseparable. She almost instantly became what I thought was the love of my life and my best friend rolled into one. We were both doing A-level art and the teachers rather stupidly left us to work alone in the art block in the evenings. We used to go up to the top of the building and snog; I may have even groped a boob once, but we didn't go any further. I would only let myself snog her because of her boyfriend, who was still on the scene. Yes, I know it was wrong, but I was infatuated.

We almost became like brother and sister – who snogged. We were so close that if ever a teacher wanted to find one of us, instead of saying, 'Where's Ollie?' or 'Where's Tilly?' they would say, 'Where are Ollie and Tilly?'

Nothing else mattered to me; not work, not teachers, just her. She was such a rebel. She used to listen to blink-182 and wear cropped tops and miniskirts. It was 2004 and that was rebellious and very cool, I'll have you know. It might not sound very risqué, but to someone in a Quaker boarding school in the middle of a country village, that was rebellious. Whenever teachers used to tell her off for basically wearing no clothes, she would stare blankly at them, ask if they had finished and then walk off. She didn't give a toss, and I adored her for it. At this point, I was still dressing in my skater-boy style, but I later discovered my love of fashion through a new friend, Tululla.

Tululla was an amazing girl. Her mother had recently died and left her with three godparents: Cath Kidston, Julien Macdonald, and Christian Louboutin. She certainly got better Christmas presents than I ever did. So that October we went to London to stay with Cath Kidston at her home for the whole of Fashion Week. I knew I had to look cool so I wore jeans and some brand-new Converse, and I wrapped a shoelace around my wrist several times so it looked like a bracelet. Tilly told me to do it. I turned up at Julien Macdonald's show wearing what I thought was a real statement top that said 'Michael Jackson is innocent' on the front. Then some bitch walked in wearing a T-shirt with the words 'Camilla for Queen' emblazoned across the front, and I was furious that she'd stolen my near-paparazzi thunder.

Being surrounded by all these people gave me yet another taste of what I wanted my life to be in the future. It made me much more aware of fashion and I started to develop my own style even more and take risks with what I wore. Not always successfully, I hasten to add.

That trip wasn't without its low points, however. Julien invited us along to the after-show party at a club called Tantra. They were all so kind to me and treated me as if I was family. Talulla was 18 by then, but I had to lie to Julien and use fake ID to get into the club.

We were sat at a table when Rachel Stevens from, at that time, S Club 7 fame, came and sat down with us. She had just broken up with her long-term boyfriend Jeremy Edwards and she was so unbelievably hot.

I was smoking Vogue cigarettes as I thought they were very cool (looking back, I couldn't have looked more gay), and began trying to chat her up. After several large glasses of wine I was convinced she'd be interested in a 17-year-old virgin with little or no prospects.

When I was going through a shit time at Embley during my disastrous exams I always used to listen to S Club 7's 'Reach For The Stars' because the lyrics were inspirational, which I remember telling her. What. A. Dick. She was very sweet and smiled as I rambled on, and a part of me honestly thought I was in there with her. I quite obviously wasn't.

We stayed with Julien that night and he suggested we all headed to this club he loved. I was very excited about going to another London club. After several vodkas I went to the loo, where all these guys were smiling at me. I couldn't understand it. Unless ... they all fancied me? Maybe I was a hit with the gays even though dating a man wasn't something I was thinking about back then. Then I looked down and realised that I was weeing onto an enormous mirror so that the entire bathroom could see my willy. They found it hilarious that I hadn't noticed.

I was so naïve. As I nervously ran out of the loo some random guy walked up to me and said, 'Charlie?' I politely reached out my hand and said, 'No, I'm called Ollie.' He rolled his eyes and said, 'No, I mean, do you want some cocaine?' Oh dear. I politely declined and hurried back to find Tululla, burning with embarrassment. Clearly I had a lot to learn.

Until that point the only celebrity I'd ever seen was Lily Savage in panto at the Southampton Mayflower, so it was an unbelievable experience to meet all of those famous people. I wasn't starstruck, but I loved it. I loved the whole world, and I knew that I had to do everything I could to be part of it.

CHAPTER 8

BAD INFLUENCE

For the entire time I was at Sidford, Tilly drove me slightly mad because she wouldn't/couldn't be with me as she was still in a secure long-term relationship with her boyfriend, Finn. I used to cry myself to sleep in my dorm over my feelings for her and every day I hurt a little bit more. I know she would never have upset me intentionally, she just didn't know how strongly I felt about her.

The longer I knew her, the harder it became for me not to be with her. It was like we were in a relationship, but at the same time we weren't. We spent every moment together, but it never went further than the occasional snog in secret or hand-holding as friends (you know when you swing your joined hands back and forth? For me it was the only way I could hold her hand without it seeming weird).

I'm not sure she was even that happy with Finn. I think she was so secure with his family and the whole set up that she couldn't see a life without him.

Weirdly, in time, Finn and I ended up becoming good friends and I used to go and stay at his house sometimes. I felt terribly guilty about the fact that I had been snogging his girlfriend behind his back, and worried that if he ever found out he would beat me up.

I knew it wasn't right but I thought I loved her. There was a very thin line for me between the guilt I felt and my obsession. My obsession almost masked my guilt because I had such strong feelings for her.

Despite the angst I felt, the three of us used to hang out a lot, along with another girl from school: Annabel.

One Friday evening we were all out at a pub near Finn's parents' house. I was trying to be cool and drink pints of beer with Finn. At that point in my life I don't think I'd ever drunk more than one pint and I hated them. It tasted like someone had taken a perfectly good glass of water, farted in it and put it back in the fridge for later. But I wanted to look like a proper lad.

For some reason, Finn decided that it would be hilarious to have a foursome that night. My entire world came to a halt. So the boyfriend of the girl I was in love with, wanted me to have sex with her in front of him. Only one problem: I was a fucking virgin. I was terrified at the thought of having sex, let alone the fact that if I were to do it with Tilly it would inevitably last little more than a few minutes. I knew I would have to think about something disgusting to stop myself finishing early, but I couldn't think what. Seriously, start accumulating things in your mind that you want to think of, like your granny pooing or Susan Boyle's cat. At the same time I was very, very excited.

After the pub closed we started walking back to Finn's house. The girls were walking a few steps in front, giggling and whispering, while Finn and I held back to discuss what was going to happen when we got back. All of a sudden my stomach started churning and I knew I was going to throw up. Maybe it was a mixture of beer and nerves but there was no way of holding it in. Finn turned to me and hissed, 'Don't throw up. If you're sick, the girls won't want to shag us.'

Somehow I managed to projectile vomit onto some grass while still walking so the girls didn't suspect a thing. To be honest, I can't even remember if I brushed my teeth when I got home, I was so nervous.

Back in Finn's bedroom we awkwardly slumped onto the beds that had been made up on the floor by Finn's mum, and started fumbling around. Instead of concentrating on Finn, Tilly immediately started kissing and straddling me. I looked over and I could see that Annabel was sitting on top of Finn, but he couldn't take his eyes off us.

Things got quite serious and Tilly and I were moments away from having sex – at last! We were both naked, she was on top of me, and her boyfriend knew all about it. What could go wrong?! Then suddenly Finn leapt up, turned the lights on and went crazy jealous. I ended the night half naked, still a virgin, with the girl I wanted more than anyone sloping off to bed with her boyfriend. That was my first, and last, foursome, and it certainly didn't go as I'd hoped.

My time at Sibford was quite a strange one. On one hand it was awful because I was constantly heartbroken over Tilly, but on the other it was great because I was away from everything I was used to. I was living in the middle of the countryside and I had much less academic pressure as I had chosen all vocational subjects.

I even joined the rugby team for a week. I know it's hard to imagine me roughing it out in the mud, but Tilly's travel and tourism class overlooked rugby practice so I thought it would be a good way to impress her. In the end I decided that getting beaten up by 15 guys in the faint hope that she would watch me catch a ball was not worth it.

Around this time, I became good friends with an openly gay guy named Jeff from the local village. I was so messed up about Tilly and used to go for long walks during which I would speak to him about my relationship problems, and how desperately I wanted to be with Tilly. One night, something quite strange happened. We were both having a cigarette and laughing and having fun and then suddenly we were kissing. I was so taken aback because I wasn't expecting it. I had certainly found certain guys attractive in the past, but I thought that all men appreciated a good-looking guy in the same way they appreciate girls they fancy. But this was totally different.

For starters, it felt very alien kissing someone with stubble. I was confused about Tilly and now to add to everything, was there a chance I liked guys? This was the last thing I needed. It was just a one-off occurrence, and something that Jeff and I never really spoke about again, but by the time my second year at Sibford came to a close I was feeling very confused about relationships in general. So, I did what every 18-year-old boy does (but doesn't tell anyone about): I went home to Southampton and cried on my mother's shoulder.

It was a Saturday night. We opened a bottle of wine, smoked and talked about how shit love lives can be. This is the relationship I have with my mother, and I never want it to change. I also wouldn't be sat here right now, on my bed in London, writing this book, or even be on *Made in Chelsea* had it not been for what happened that evening.

I was slumped on the sofa, post-tears, maybe gay, watching TV with an empty bottle of wine in front of me when my friend Stef called and demanded that I go to our local club, Jesters, with her, which is simultaneously the best and worst club I have ever been to. It's got a sticky floor and dodgy lights and the most expensive drink you can buy is about £2. When you're a student, it's an absolute dream. I was feeling quite down and so I flatly refused to leave the comfort of the sofa and my mother's arms. But then I realised how ridiculous that sounded, so I got off the sofa, got dressed and headed out.

I walked in to a rammed bar and could see Stef dancing away to 'Love Shack' and getting rather close to a guy who looked like Phil Collins (just your type, Binky). To the right of her I spotted my godmother's sons, Jack and Tom, who I went on holiday with to Vale do Lobo, where I met Hattie Clark. It turned out they were out partying with two friends – a girl that we shall call Jesters Girl and her friend Seb, who they'd met on holiday in Portugal. Jesters Girl was my age, very pretty and was in the last month of A-levels at a very posh private girls' school in London. For the first time in ages, I felt a flutter in my heart (and pants). I finally fancied someone other than Tilly.

It only took five Jager Bombs to build up the courage to try to get a snog, but I managed it as we leant against the bar with the *Baywatch* theme tune blaring out in the background.

Jesters Girl told me she had to go back to London in the morning, and in my infinite wisdom (or perhaps drunken stupor) I decided to pretend I had to be in London the following day too, so I could spend some more time with her.

When I awoke the next morning, it still felt like a great idea, and I was on half term so there was nothing to stop me escaping for the day. I met her at the train station feeling very perky; I'm fairly certain I was still pissed. We talked all the way on the train and I kept wondering how I was going to blag the fact that I barely knew my way around London, let alone had any business being there. I had only visited on school trips or with Slowen's mum, so I decided to follow her lead and go wherever she was.

That was the first day I ever set foot in Chelsea. I remember falling in love with it immediately. It was a beautiful day and Jesters Girl and I walked around for hours, sat outside the Royal Court Theatre, talked about life and watched all of the beautiful people walking by. After saying a painful goodbye to my new love I went home and decided that one day soon, I was going to build a life in London.

Jesters Girl and I stayed in touch and started seeing each other, and a few weekends later I drove my little green Ford Fiesta to Datchet in Berkshire, where Jesters Girl had invited me to meet some of her male friends at Eton College's annual Fourth of June gathering. This traditional date in the calendar is like an open day, speech day and sports day rolled into one, and all the Eton parents go along and watch rowing, get drunk and eat from Fortnum & Mason hampers out of the back of their Range Rovers.

When the time came to say goodbye to Jesters Girl I really didn't want to leave – I felt like I was starting to fall for her in a big way. I was halfway down the M3 to Southampton when I realised that I *really* didn't want to leave her, so I turned the car around and drove to London to find her at her school.

I don't know what came over me, other than it felt like I had no other purpose in life but to find her and be with her that night. When I arrived at her school, I phoned her to tell her how I felt and thankfully she said she felt the same. She told me to wait in the car while she'd sneak out. It was quite late so she stuffed pillows under her duvet to make it look as though she was sleeping, and her best friend – who we will call London Girl – promised to cover for her if any of the teachers came by after lights out.

She climbed out of her dorm window, ran across the sports field and got into my car, then we drove off in the direction of my home in Southampton, thrilled to be doing something so forbidden. It was 3am before we arrived home. My mum was out for the night so we crept up the stairs, both knowing and not knowing at the same time how that night would end. With hushed voices, the occasional giggle and a lot of groping blindly in the dark, finally that night

– after many painful teenage years praying it would happen – I lost my virginity. The moment that I had waited for for so long had come. So to speak.

We were both so inexperienced and I had to work very hard that night as it was all so new. I remember having to think about keeping myself erect. My condom was labelled 'extra small, for the more modest gentleman' – I have no idea why they were in my house (thanks, Mum), but they made me look like a right dick. I'm surprised they didn't cut off my valuable blood supply.

I thought back to my sterile school sex lessons and carefully played back the moment where they taught us how to open the condom packet. We were warned not to bite it in case we broke the condom inside without realising, and to hold the tip so the air bubble disappears. It's all very technical when you're in the moment. Then I was good to go, as it were.

I don't remember there being any form of foreplay and I won't pretend I knew what I was doing, but for some reason it seemed to last forever.

As soon as we had finished Jesters Girl started to hyperventilate. I like to think it was because she'd never seen such a big willy but I think other things were to blame, to be honest. I was terrified I had killed her. I went at it a bit like a wild jack rabbit because I thought that was the best way to do it. 'Just fucking thrust,' I told myself. Who knew you were meant to start slowly? I think the poor girl was exhausted. It wasn't the best start to my sexual encounters.

Morning came and I woke as a new, sexually experienced person. After a triumphant, post-coital cuddle in bed, and after hurriedly tidying away my virginity condom wrapper into my sex time capsule, Jesters Girl very sweetly offered to make breakfast wearing only a shirt and my boxer shorts.

Because my mother was working on the BBC Breakfast programme she was usually out of the house until midday. But as luck would have it, not that day. She came home early to be confronted by a nearly naked 18-year-old stranger making toast in her kitchen.

After some embarrassing introductions, Jesters Girl got dressed and I drove her back to school. My sex life may have got off to a rocky start, but at least there was finally *a* sex life to speak of and the girl I had lost my virginity to was wonderful, kind, beautiful and very clever. I was happy to say she was my first.

I went back to school to tell my friends that I had finally become a man. For the first time in my life I could drive, have sex and love and I felt just like Peter Pan must have done when he realised he could fly, fight and crow.

I told Ed, my best guy friend at school, first. He put his hand on my shoulder and said 'Good lad.' Ed was a bit like Jay from *The Inbetweeners* in that he always made out that he'd had loads of sex in loads of different places, so he acted very nonchalantly as if it wasn't a big deal.

Of course, I also told Tilly, who was distinctly unimpressed. Even though she was in a relationship herself I don't think she liked hearing about my sexual exploits, no matter how few there were. I even told my mum, because I've always told her everything, and she was terribly unfazed and congratulated me but just told me to be careful.

My mum was all about promoting safe sex. Tragically, her brother Mark died of AIDS when I was two years old. He was very much a part of the 80s gay club scene and used to go out with a famous 80s pop star, and it was around the time when AIDS was constantly in the press but remained a much-misunderstood disease.

As a result of his illness Uncle Mark was never allowed to hold me, and the thought of that breaks my heart. I wish I'd had the chance to get to know him better.

I thought of him a lot around the time when I came out as being bisexual because he's someone I would love to have spoken to about it. Losing Uncle Mark like that has made it really important to me that I support HIV charities and help people understand the illness more.

Losing my uncle so young and amongst the hysteria that surrounded AIDS at the time, I always assumed that it was much easier to catch than it is. Every time I cut myself I used to panic that I had HIV, and between the ages of 15 to around 18 I convinced myself that I was HIV positive. To tell you the absolute truth, that's the sole reason I didn't let Lucie go down on me in the hallway that night. I used to research HIV constantly because it absolutely terrified me. Every time I got a small rash I thought it was a sign that I was dying. I'm not making light of it in any way, because it was a truly terrifying time. I was young and I believed the misinformation.

As I got older I came to my senses and found out the truth about HIV and AIDS. I guess I just got more educated and less scared.

My mum had such a militant attitude to condoms as a result of her brother's tragic death that she delegated a drawer in the bathroom of our house exclusively to condoms so that my sister and I had access to them at any time. This was before I was even having sex! Come to think of it, my first STI check was before I had even had sex – that made the nurses at the clinic scratch their heads a little! I think I was only about 13 when Mum came up with the idea of the condom drawer. She obviously had high hopes for me.

Much like a sweetie drawer, the condom drawer wasn't just for our use either; all of my friends were allowed to come round and help themselves when they needed to. When you're a teenager, going into a shop to buy condoms is one of the most mortifying things you can do, and Mum's view was that she would rather provide them and know that my friends were safe, than have them act irresponsibly.

Although Jesters Girl sadly didn't end up becoming the love of my life, our relationship was an important milestone in my love life and she will always have a special place in my heart. There wasn't a big drama or break-up, we just spoke and texted less and less, and it became obvious that neither of us wanted to be in a full-on relationship with the other.

I will always be proud to call her my first, and grateful for the educational experience that she gave me. But it wasn't to be, and I was ready for the next chapter in my sexual adventure.

♥ DEAR OLLIE: LOSING YOUR ♥ VIRGINITY

When it comes to losing your virginity, I have eight simple pieces of advice:

1. When you do it, do it slowly; don't act like you're speeding towards a finishing line.
2. Do it nicely; then they might want to come back for more.
3. Don't boast about it to your friends. There's no way he/she'll want to see you again if you've made him/her sound bad.
4. Try to do it somewhere nice with someone you care about. Don't do it in a bathtub drunk at a party with a stranger. I know one girl who lost her virginity when she was at a fancy dress party dressed as one of the Jackson 5, and although it's a funny story to tell, it wasn't exactly a beautiful moment.
5. For all you men, always have an image in your head that will prevent you from finishing early. I always think of David Dickinson. Never use your mum as an image. There is nothing more horrific than seeing your mum's face when you're having sex and you're past the point of no return.
6. Also, I cannot stress enough the importance of condoms. It's not just about protecting yourself from

pregnancy, STDs can ruin your life. I can't tell you how many of my friends have had chlamydia, and unless you get tested you don't know you've got it, so you can pass it on to other people.

7. A tip for girls, don't pull a willy too hard. I have had to ask a few girls to be a bit gentler over the years. It's not a Shake Weight.

8. You're best to stick to missionary for your first time, just to be on the safe side. You don't have to throw each other around the room in order to have a good time. You can save all of that for later!

CHAPTER 9

THE SEX DOOR INTO CAMBRIDGE

After Jesters Girl and I drifted apart, I was ready to get back on the dating scene. It was fairly obvious that Tilly wasn't going to leave Finn and I rather liked the idea of going on a proper date for the first time ever.

I would imagine that 99 per cent of the time it's the guys who are doing the asking when it comes to dates, and in my opinion, men should *always* pay on the first date. It's nice if a girl offers to go halves, but I think that if you make the effort to ask someone out, you should also find a nice venue and treat her to dinner. Don't even get me started on the girls who don't say thank you – that is a deal breaker – nor on the etiquette of gay dating and who pays. Who's meant to know? I'll go into more detail about that later.

If you are going on a date always, always make sure you have a back-up credit card with you. Imagine if your card gets declined when you're paying for the meal or drinks. Could there be anything more mortifying?

First dates can either be amazing or hideous. There is one date I went on that I am still mortified about. It was way back in my Tilly-obsessed sixth form days, pre Jesters Girl.

Every Sunday night I had to travel from Southampton to Banbury to go back to school, and on one such evening I got off the train to discover a group of girls, who were about 17, waiting on the platform. I could tell from their enormous blonde hair and pashminas that they went to the girls' school nearby.

We all used the same cab driver, an incredible guy called Ritchie, who looked like Chris Moyles. He used to pick us up from the station and drive us to our respective schools. I was first in line for Ritchie to pick me up when I got talking to the five Sloaney girls, and I offered them the cab before me.

When Ritchie got back 10 minutes later he handed me five phone numbers the girls had given him, and told me to take my pick. It was by far the coolest thing since the foursome! I felt like Ryan Reynolds.

There was one girl in particular that I liked – we shall call her McFly Girl. Ritchie told me she was defi- nitely single because she'd just broken up with Harry from McFly (hence the name), who happened to be my hair icon Charlie from Busted's best friend. We were a match made in heaven. She was clearly the coolest girl in her school, so I plucked up the courage to text her and we engaged in some light flirting. After a bit of banter, I asked if I could take her out on a date, which she accepted. The only trouble was, Banbury wasn't the coolest place to take out someone who had just broken up with a rock star. There was either a McDonald's or Abrakebabra, a kebab shop boasting the best doner in Banbury. So I decided to take her to a pub in Oxford called The Goose.

She turned up at the pub in a brand-new convertible mini with her best friend Jemma, who it has to be said had the biggest boobs of anyone I've ever seen in my entire life. Forget Candy or Tiffany, these were bespoke bra stuff. Unfortunately, the drunker I got, the more I kept staring at them. I thought I was being quite subtle about it and in my head the date was going really well. But McFly Girl sadly wasn't thinking the same thing and kept on catching me staring. Now, I got pissed, really pissed, like two-bottles-of-wine-at-18 pissed.

She offered to drop me off at school as she hadn't been drinking, and on the journey back I put my hand over hers as she changed gears and slurred, 'I really like you.' It seemed the kind of gesture a girl would want. She smiled weakly, dropped me off and we never saw each other again. Hot tip: if you're going on a date, don't get so pissed that you stare at your date's friend's enormous boobs.

Funnily enough, I bumped into McFly Girl recently at a party and she gave me a kiss and said, 'We were the relationship that never happened.' I think she was drunker than I was this time. I was tempted to ask her how Jemma was but I thought I might be pushing my luck.

On the whole, I would say that getting really drunk on dates can be useful, but only if they're not that attractive. It can of course lead to disaster too, but at least you can blame it on the alcohol. I'm actually really quite a good drunk because I generally know when to stop and I don't start slobbering over people, but I certainly wouldn't have snogged some of the girls I have had I not had a few drinks first. Some of them I would rather forget about too.

With only eight weeks to go until the end of sixth form at Sibford I became increasingly rebellious with my newfound dating and mating confidence. We were the oldest pupils in the school so we felt like we ran the place, as any sixth former does. We wanted our last summer schooldays to be as enjoyable as possible.

I lived in the sixth-form house, where the girls slept on one side and the boys on the other. There was just one door in between us that kept us apart. Clearly this story could only end in disaster ...

The connecting door was locked at 11pm each night; we all saw it as a barrier which prevented us from getting any form of action, so it was aptly called the 'Sex Door', even by our teachers.

My friend Astrid's dad had previously been a pupil at the school, and after a few glasses of wine over Sunday lunch one week he told us about a key that had been passed down through generations. It was the key that opened the Sex Door. It had existed for decades but the year before we started at the school the key was lost and apparently that was the end of that. No one had dared to replace it. I have no idea how he knew this; it certainly wasn't on the newsletter I got.

We immediately saw this as a full-scale *Lord of the Rings*-type quest. We were determined to get hold of another copy of the key to carry on the legacy of generations of ex-Sibford pupils. Thus two boys from our year, who shall remain nameless, went on a mission to steal the key from the cleaner.

Having successfully swiped it, they went straight into town, got a copy cut, and then replaced it within an hour so the cleaner was none the wiser. Frodo would have been proud.

As the oldest boy in our dorm I became the keeper of the key, the key master if you will, and I kept it safely hidden behind the frame of a picture of Rupert and me.

We took full advantage of the key and used to creep over to the other half of the building in the evenings to party with the girls. It wasn't about sex, it was just chilling with friends after lights out, and it not being allowed made it far more exciting. I used to go on booze cruises to Calais with my dad every now and then, and on these I'd buy loads of mini bottles of Moët. I'd smuggle them into the dorm, and then we'd sit on the end of each other's beds drinking champagne through straws, with the housemaster asleep downstairs.

I hid my booze, along with my cigarettes, in one of the air vents in the ceiling. The more we got away with using the key and having our nights of fun, the more careless we became. So I guess what happened next was somewhat inevitable.

My love of theatre and dramatics was still shining bright, so as I was preparing to leave Sibford I applied for a Drama foundation course in Cambridge that was run in association with RADA. It sounded like the perfect course for me to do before I put my plan to move to London into action.

I carefully filled out my application form, sent it off and kept everything crossed. I was over the moon when I got a letter inviting me for an audition. Mum and Dad both came along with me to help calm my nerves. However, just as I was about to go into the audition room my mobile rang and I answered it. *Big* mistake when I was trying to stay relaxed.

I heard Astrid's frantic voice on the other end of the phone explaining how she and her boyfriend Luke had used the Sex Key the previous night and had been caught in her room by the housemaster. He had given them an ultimatum: either they tell him who the key belonged to, or they would both be expelled. If they revealed the holder of the key, they would only be suspended and the keeper of the key would suffer the consequences. Obviously, that person was me. I told her not to worry and that we would sort something out – I could tell she was in a real state about it. I didn't know how we were going to rectify the situation, but there had to be a way. And besides, my audition was starting in a few minutes.

God knows how, but I managed to get through the audition, albeit very shakily. I had to perform a Shakespearian piece, so I chose Act I, Scene I from *Twelfth Night*. I also had to do a strange modern piece about the fact that my hair wouldn't stop growing and sing a song about the corner of the sky, which I started an octave too high. As I left the college I told my parents everything. I was still quite shaky from the audition and I must have looked terrified. I wasn't sure if they would be furious or think it was funny. Thankfully for me, it was the latter.

Astrid was in the year below me so she had another year at Sibford to go, so I told her to tell the house-master that it was me who was responsible for the Sex Key.

In the back of my mind I kept thinking that if the drama school found out I'd been expelled from school, there was no way they would let me onto the course. I was so desperate to be accepted and move to Cambridge, but equally I couldn't see Astrid expelled halfway through her A-levels. I had no choice but to tell the truth. I knew it could cost me my place at drama school – and that was such a horrible thought because I had no back-up plan whatsoever. I would have been so angry with myself if I'd thrown away an amazing opportunity for the sake of a few (admittedly very good) nights of rebellion.

After coming clean to the housemaster, the school ended up asking me to leave on the day of my last A-level. They broke the news that they were booting me out 10 minutes before I was going into my final drama exam, so I ended up giggling deliriously through the whole thing. Instead of answering a question on the topic I'd been studying I decided to write the entire essay about ballet. I'd never watched a ballet in my life but at that point I thought it was the perfect thing to do. I had reached the point where I no longer cared: school was over for me, I was done. Even though I was asked to leave, the teachers said they were very sad to see me go. The day before, I had even accepted the Dorothy Hawley Award, the main award given to a pupil who has shown outstanding care, consideration and helpfulness in the spirit of service to the community of the school. I was allowed to go along for our leavers' meal and I ended up admitting everything to the teachers about drinking booze on the school grounds and the fact we had nicknames for them. What did I have to lose? I thought they had better know it all. They just laughed.

With school now behind me for good, that 2006 summer holiday felt absolutely perfect to me. I had no responsibilities and I had even managed to land myself a place at the drama school despite being kicked out of school. When I opened the letter saying I'd been accepted I was beyond happy. It was exactly where I wanted to be and I felt really proud that I'd secured a place. I was entering a new time in my life, a more grown-up one. I was no longer a school or college pupil, I was a student. I was ready to become an actor.

My friends and I knew we would all be heading off to university after the summer, so it was our last chance to spend some quality time together before we went our separate ways.

I headed straight down to Cornwall with some guys, and when I arrived it appeared that half of Britain's public school population had the same idea. People were pitching tents all around our caravan and it was absolutely packed.

We celebrated the start of the holiday by heading to the Oyster Catcher, a pub in Polzeath that holds amazing memories for me and is always my first stop when I get to Cornwall.

As I made my way over to the bar, standing there flanked by two very cool older guys wearing beanies and tracksuit bottoms, was Hattie Clark. My beautiful

Miss Vale do Lobo. I stopped dead in my tracks, double-blinking to make sure it was her. She was older, taller and was drinking beer instead of a Squashed Frog, but it was definitely her.

I had thought about her often over the years. The photos of that summer were still on my wall, so it was such a shock to see her standing there in the flesh. I was so excited when I noticed my friends ogling her, that I really smugly announced, 'Hold on guys, she's a good friend. I had better go and say hello.'

I strutted over, anticipating our emotional reunion. In my mind, it was going to be like that scene from *Forrest Gump* – tears streaming down her face, she would leap into my arms, whereupon I'd spin her around while all those in the bar watched on in envy. But as I stood in front of her and smiled like an idiot, waiting for the scene to unfold after our three long years apart, she looked at me blankly. I started to panic and blurted out, 'Hattie, it's Ollie!' in a very unmanly high-pitched squeal. She looked at me blankly again before replying, 'Sorry, *who?*'

I was mortified. To make matters worse I smiled really excitedly and said, 'It's Ollie, from Vale do Lobo! We spent a week together three years ago!' Still nothing.

As if I didn't look enough of a twat, I followed that up with, 'I've got photos of you all over my wall!' Yes. Nice one, Ollie. Looking like stalker with a high-pitched voice is always a good way to get the girl.

Hattie looked me up and down, cocked her head to one side and, without a moment's hesitation, said, 'Well, you'd better take them down then.' Her two startlingly good-looking 6-foot-5 male companions, with their beanie hats and Adidas tracksuit bottoms, sniggered as she turned her back on me and carried on drinking her beer.

My heart sank. With a dry mouth and a sinking feeling deep in my stomach, I walked back to my friends, who had watched the whole episode. It was an utterly hideous moment. The girl I had daydreamed about for years had just slammed me down in front of a bar full of people. I went on to get very drunk that night, and tried my best to act like I didn't care. I hoped that would be the last I would ever see of Hattie and her sneering face, but sadly she came back to haunt me again. Seriously, that girl is impossible to shake off.

The rest of the holiday in Cornwall passed by in a drunken blur, though I do remember lots of snogging and even getting a mediocre hand job on the beach (pretty much using tears as lube), as I tried to shake off Hattie's very public and embarrassing rejection. I returned to Southampton determined to redeem myself – and my friend Stef's 18th birthday party was the perfect opportunity to do so.

The party was held in a fabulous house in the middle of the countryside and anyone who was anyone – well, anyone who was a teenager living in and around the Southampton area – was invited along. We all had a few drinks and got quite merry, and my friend George started snogging the best-looking girl at the party, who I will call Dorset Girl.

I was always jealous of George because he was very good-looking, owned a boat, had an amazing body and had somehow managed to gain the nickname Jumbo George, which always went down very well when meeting girls. I was still stuck with Coner Boner, although I was to earn a new nickname later that night.

That night we all ended up sleeping in a barn together, and there I started fooling around on a hay bale with a pretty girl called Clarissa. I felt like I was in an 80s porno and I had the hair to match. The next day I woke up after an evening of barn canoodling, and was having a morning wee when I noticed that something didn't look quite right downstairs. There was a small bump on my willy that looked like a scab. When I scraped it off I realised, to my horror, that on closer inspection it had arms and legs. It was a tick that I'd obviously picked up in the barn. I stupidly confided in Pugsley, who then told everyone else, which resulted in me being called 'Tick Dick' for the next year. I'm relieved to say that I've lived that one down now. Ollie 'Coner Boner' 'Tick Dick' Locke doesn't easily roll off the tongue. It's no Jumbo George.

My departure for drama school was soon on the horizon, but I was determined to pack in as much fun as possible before I had to knuckle down in the real world. It was one of the last parties of the summer, which my friend Stef was driving us to. As I climbed into the back of her car I was greeted by her very hot cousin, who turned out to be Dorset Girl. She was the same girl I had very enviously watched George snog at Stef's tick-dick bash.

Dorset Girl was gorgeous, hilarious and a lot of fun. She had long blonde hair flicked over to one side, and said 'yah' instead of 'yeah'. I thought she was wonderful.

She had just come out of a two-year relationship with a guy called Jasper and she was on the rebound. Of course instead of that putting me off I decided that night would be the ideal opportunity to make my move.

We all ended up drinking a lot and sleeping on makeshift beds on the floor of the birthday girl's house. She came and slept next to me and under the shadow of darkness, we started snogging. Awkwardly, Jasper, who was at the same party, decided it would be a great idea to come and sleep the other side of her, like some great protector. He clearly wasn't over her, but the fact that she slept facing me gave me all the evidence I needed that she was definitely well on her way to getting over him.

I asked to see Dorset Girl again, and soon we were practically living in each other's pockets. She was in her last year of sixth form at a boarding school in – funnily enough – Dorset, about 20 minutes from where her parents lived, so I would travel to see her whenever she could escape from school. It was an innocent but full-on, 18-year-old love. We would make CDs of songs for each other and go on picnics, snogging the entire time.

We'd walk for miles around the Dorset hills with the dogs all snuggled up together, and then get back to her house, tired but happy. Her mum would cook us a Sunday roast and we'd all sit around the dinner table chatting over wine. In retrospect I think Dorset Girl was my first *real* love. Up until that point I thought I'd been in love with Tilly, but being with Dorset Girl made me realise that you can't truly be in love with someone when you know they don't love you back. What Dorset Girl and I had was perfect. Or so I thought.

♥ DEAR OLLIE: FIRST DATE ♥ RULES

So you've finally managed to grab a date with someone who is quite funny and not completely unfortunate-looking – and in fact in the right light looks like they might be quite good in bed. The only problem is you haven't done much dating recently, so you just don't know the rules. In this case you need to call up your sluttiest friend and find out the lowdown on the dating scene. Where do you go? Who pays? How far do you go with them on the first night?

- So, beforehand, always make sure you look good with your clothes off. Your intentions may always be innocent, but if your date happens to declare that they are in fact a billionaire and are flying you to Brazil for the evening, the last thing you want is to have an Amazonian jungle growing downstairs (men, that goes for you too!).
- Remember that the image you project on that first date will either give you a pass to another date or to another three months of watching films alone, so always dress wonderfully. Girls, try to be a tiny bit seductive – it's even better if you don't give him anything, because then he'll want you all the more.

- Eye contact is key; don't stare, but looking right into their eyes is very sexy and you will find you can control the situation through eye contact.
- Be confident (particularly the guys), but I always find that if you show a tiny bit of vulnerability you might be surprised at the response you get. I have a friend who, after a few bottles of wine, would tell their date how bad his childhood was, which apparently worked every time. Don't do it on that level, but just give them a glimpse of a weakness.
- Comedy is the way to *any* girl's heart. Everyone loves to laugh and you will be surprised at how powerful an aphrodisiac that is. So guys, get on a comedy course …
- Now the greeting and the goodbye are always difficult. Always stick to a kiss on the cheek at least – shaking their hand will only ever give the wrong impression. When it comes to the goodbye, you should know what to do, depending on how well the date went. If you know it went like a Shakespeare sonnet, go in for the kiss – you've probably shared a bottle of wine by then, so just go for it. If it went horribly, say it was lovely and make a quick exit.
- Girls, in my eyes, if the guy has asked you on the date then they should pay! Always offer, I repeat *always* make the gesture of getting your card out, but you should not be expected to pay. If they make you pay half on a first date, you need to rethink this one.

Me, aged one. I'm already perfecting my photo face.

Me and my sister Amelia as kids. Check out Postman Pat on the left. He's never looked so terrifying.

Milk? Pass me the bloody champagne! Obviously my taste for Chelsea life started young.

My wonderful mum and dad. Yes, I know, I look nothing like them. Perhaps Dad should get a spray tan?

Excited about my first day at school, aged four. Am I wearing ballet pumps?

On holiday in Vale do Lobo. This photo is solid proof that the infamous Hattie Clarke and I were friends (and it's still got Blue Tack on the back!).

Dressed as Superman at *that* party. I'm grateful the photo doesn't show the red thong, stuffed with a cricket box!

Aged 18, at the beginning of my long hair phase (and ridiculous facial expressions).

A CD Dorset Girl made for me. I can't understand why she put 'You're So Vain' on there. Or 'Swing Low', come to mention it . . .

With Shakespeare, my post-Dorset Girl break-up rabbit. I have never looked uglier.

My school report for Design and Technology – clearly a career in woodwork wasn't for me.

Enjoying a barbecue with friends on a beach in Cornwall, aged 19. Cornwall will always have a special place in my heart.

Mine and Pugsley's initials scratched into a bench in Port Quinn, Cornwall. Yes, they're still there!

Cowes Week, where I first met Richard Dinan (*second from left*). Clearly, the sea air was doing wonders for my hair.

Double the fun! Me hanging out with the cardboard cutout I made for London Girl. Perhaps not one of my sanest ideas.

The front cover of Richard's magazine, *Ammunition*, for which Millie did the make-up. My friend Antalya is wearing the short gold dress and her brother Alex, my old flat mate, is holding the flag.

Rocking a headset while working the door at Maggie's, a nightclub in Chelsea.

A night out with Richard (*far right*) at 151
on the King's Road, my second home.

Working the door at 151 (*left*) and hailing a taxi on my way
home (*right*). Pretty much a standard evening at work.

With my girls, Binky and Cheska. What would I do without them?

The first night Gabriella and I met – and *those* hair extensions.

With Binky, Cheska and Gabriella on a skiing holiday the week before Gabs and I broke up.

(Ian West/PA Archive/Press Association Images)

At the Harry Potter premiere. Don't believe
the smile, I was bloody terrified!

Living the dream – with Jennifer
Saunders at the BAFTA after-show
party. Jennifer, the offer to be
in *Ab Fab* still stands!

Hanging out with Verne
Troyer. How surreal my life
has become.

CHAPTER 10

'YOU'RE JUST TOO NICE'

———

By mid-September 2006 I was due to start drama school in Cambridge, so Dorset Girl and I said the first horrible goodbye of many. We both cried our eyes out.

I was really excited about starting at Cambridge, but I was also very happy in my relationship and she was a big part of my life. I wished she was coming with me. She was 17, a year below me and still at school, so she wasn't able to visit me like she could if she was at uni, so it was hard.

It wasn't a huge deal for me moving away from home because I had been used to boarding school, so, despite missing Dorset Girl terribly, I settled into Cambridge life very quickly. I loved the place and I remember being very impressed that it had the famous Nando's because I'd never been to one before.

I did my first ever proper food shop, admittedly at M&S with my dad's credit card so I guess buying hummus and olives wasn't exactly what you'd call your usual student experience.

It was at Cambridge that I also began to experiment with fake tan. Having grown up in a house with my mum and sister, I'd watched them put on make-up and suddenly become better-looking as a result. I saw no reason why I couldn't do the same. I've always wondered why, if men are good-looking, they wouldn't cover up the massive spot they've got from a big night out or pluck their eyebrows to make themselves look better. If girls can wear make-up, why on earth can't men? With this in mind, I started wearing my mum's Touche Éclat, but it was too light for me and made me look as if I'd been wearing large goggles while sunbathing. After several weeks of looking like a sunkissed raccoon I decided that it wasn't for me.

I saved up my money (OK, I used the credit card), went to Boots and bought a darker concealer that did the trick perfectly. I'm sure Dad would have been delighted. Then I started experimenting with the fake tan.

I'm quite olive-skinned naturally, but I also have quite a grey complexion. It's like I'm half Mediterranean, half old man. Because of that I tend to look slightly dead without any fake tan.

After all, if there's one thing that makes pretty much everyone look hotter, it's a tan. If everyone fake tanned, the world would be a better-looking place. Except redheads; they look amazing the way they are.

Anyway, my drama course was very energetic and every morning to start the day we had to do a warm-up to 'I Predict A Riot' by the Kaiser Chiefs, which involved us running around the room as fast as we could, with a hangover. We also had to do miming exercises with our Polish teacher, Kasha, where we had to pretend to be abstract things like a cloud or an embryo. I thought it was absolute bollocks but I'm sure it must have taught me something.

We had to do eight hours of ballet a week and I was absolutely shit at it. I had to wear a leotard and tights and needless to say I felt completely ridiculous. Me and one of my course friends, Gabby, who was bit of a clown, literally and metaphorically (more on her later) used to sit at the back of the class laughing. I dreaded every class, but there was no opting out of things you didn't enjoy.

Even though life in Cambridge was amazing, as soon as Friday afternoon arrived each week I would drive three hours to Dorset Girl's parents' house so we could spend those two special nights together. We were still infatuated with each other.

Dorset Girl's family was incredible. If I had to choose any parents to look after me apart from my own, it would be them. They are kind, loving, under-standing and very young at heart. They owned a house in Barbados and after a couple of months of being together I was invited to join the family for a week on the island.

On the first night we all watched the sun set, drank amazing wine and listened to James Blunt. Don't laugh – he was very cool then. One by one the guests left the table, leaving only Dorset Girl and me. She grabbed me by the hand and led me upstairs and onto the roof of the house. The view was incredible and you couldn't have asked for a more romantic setting.

Up until that point things had been quite innocent between Dorset Girl and me. But that night, in the most perfect surroundings, we had sex for the first time under the island stars. It was the first time I'd been that intimate with anyone since Jesters Girl.

It was all so dreamy as we gazed lovingly into each other's eyes. The sex was going well; I had learned my lesson about not being a jack rabbit and managed to slow it down. I felt like I'd lost my virginity all over again. We were both lying there, post-coital bliss, when we realised that the condom had split. Excellent.

The likelihood of Dorset Girl being pregnant was virtually zero, but we knew we still had to go to a pharmacy the next day to get the morning-after pill to be on the safe side.

The whole scenario was ridiculous as we tried to tell the pharmacist in hushed tones and very bad

Bajan what we wanted. It felt like we were acting out the pregnancy test skiing scene in *Bridget Jones*. I'm pretty sure everyone knew exactly what we were doing, despite me trying to distract them by taking great interest in the lollipop display on the counter.

Split condoms aside, my relationship with Dorset Girl was still the best and most fun one I'd ever had. We never argued and we treated one another amazingly. I used to send her packages down from Cambridge each week with all sorts of gifts in them, and we would never have dreamt of cheating on each other.

Dorset Girl went on the Pill after our little slip up, but I think back now and realise that even at the age of 18, I still had no idea about sex.

I spent my first proper Valentine's night with Dorset Girl when I whisked her away to Paris for two nights. Hilariously, I had to get a note from her parents giving me permission to take her out of the country so it didn't look like I was abducting her as she was 17 and I was 18. On the Eurostar, Dorset Girl started to feel unwell but I soldiered on and ordered champagne to our room using my dad's credit card and was all set for a fabulous couple of days.

My grand plan was to take her to Johnny Depp's restaurant, but I totally forgot to book it and obviously with it being the most romantic night of the year in the world's most romantic city, I couldn't get a table anywhere for dinner. We ended up in a dreadful steak shack, so it wasn't quite the classical music, gazing-across-the-table extravaganza I'd anticipated.

Dorset Girl was ill throughout the whole holiday and then on the final day it was my turn. We went up the Eiffel Tower and my meal started repeating on me in the worst possible way. There's nothing more romantic than Valentine's Day in Paris with chronic diarrhoea.

It continued all the way home, and as much as I wanted to try and make the end of the trip special, it's hard to cuddle up to someone when you're running to the train loo every couple of minutes. Damn steak tartare.

I've since learned that when you try to do romantic gestures it tends to go wrong. I much prefer to do things on a whim. Somehow they always work out so much better that way.

I can't help but think Valentine's Day is crap. There, I've said it. I have done for years and I can't see anything changing my mind in the future. It's probably only due to me being bitter because I tend to be single when every Valentine's Day comes around and so I mostly spend the most romantic night of the year with a Kleenex as my date. However, most importantly, at least Kleenex and I both believe in monogamy. If you're single, Valentine's Day is generally awful because everyone else is incredibly smug about the bouquet they're carrying home on the train from work. And if you're in a relationship, it's just a whole load of pressure to make sure she has an amazing night topped off with the best shag she's ever had. I don't understand why one night of the year needs to be more important than another. If you like someone, I think you should do lovely things because you want to, not because you feel like you should (another excuse).

The only upside is that if you're a guy trying to pull, Valentine's Day is the easiest night in the world. There are women all over the country who are going out with their friends just to get laid.

Meanwhile I was still studying in Cambridge, and although drama school was amazing, it was also bloody hard work. We used to start at 7am every morning and finish at 8pm, having done a full day of physical theatre and dance classes. Anyone who has been to drama school knows how tough it is, but I didn't mind because I loved it. I was training in the original Footlights, a room that had in the past been graced by the presence of amazing people such as Hugh Laurie, Stephen Fry and Rowan Atkinson when they were at Cambridge University, so I didn't take any of it for granted.

Despite its star-studded connections, Footlights was a small, dingy little room in the middle of Roundchurch Street in Cambridge. The parks surrounding it are so beautiful, though, and I used to spend my free time punting and cycling everywhere. I have never been happier than when I was there – especially when Dorset Girl used to come to stay for weekends.

All of the people on my course had access to Cambridge University, so I got to hear some incredible people speak. I saw Stephen Hawking do several lectures, which were phenomenal.

I was living in halls called Tripos Court, next door to a guy called Pedro, who was on a fashion design course. He was a very beautiful Italian man and, I later weirdly found out, is the best friend of Mark Francis from *Made in Chelsea*.

He and I became great friends and I used to go to his room and drink wine and smoke cigarettes most nights with another mate of ours, Natalie. We covered Pedro's smoke sensor with a condom to stop it going off, which I've always thought was rather clever, although not ideal if there's ever a fire, or an urgent need for contraception, obviously.

We used to get so trashed that I'd fall asleep in his bed most nights. He was gay, but nothing ever happened between us. It was completely platonic. I was still working out how I felt about men in general when it came to romance, and thankfully he didn't have any feelings for me. Or so I thought.

One day he knocked on my bedroom door and pulled down a piece of gauze on his arm to reveal a tattoo of my name. It said 'Ollie14', because 14 was his lucky number. It was a pretty hefty clue.

Needless to say things got a little awkward between us once I realised how much he liked me, and even more so when he told me he was in love with me. It was such a shame that it affected our friendship because I thought he was wonderful, but only as a friend. We never really got back on track after that.

I was exhausted a lot of the time because my course was so intense. I was also staying up late drinking wine with friends most evenings, then travelling down to see Dorset Girl on Friday nights, which really wore me out.

I was pretty skint too, because the petrol for a weekly return drive to Dorset cost a small fortune and I was only allowed to spend so much on my dad's emergency credit card. But it was worth it to see Dorset Girl.

After six months of dating I thought we were closer than ever. One blustery February Sunday evening I drove her back to school with her mum. I got out of the car to say goodbye, expecting us to exchange the usual 'I'll miss you's', but instead she told me very bluntly that we could no longer be together. There had been absolutely no warning signs and we'd just spent what I thought was a lovely weekend together.

I wasn't expecting it at all and I was so devastated that I felt like I was going to throw up. I tried to stop myself from crying but it was impossible. As I stood outside her boarding house looking at her with tears in my eyes, I asked her why. Her reply? 'Because you're too nice.' I couldn't believe she was actually saying those words. I thought we had an amazing future ahead of us, and yet she was dumping me for being too kind and caring. It just didn't make sense.

I could tell from the look on her face that there was no point trying to reason with her, so I walked away and got back into her mum's car. I was crying my heart out all the way back to their house. I look back now and cringe about what her mum must have thought. That day, I learned one of the most annoying but true lessons about girls. Is there *really* such a thing as being too nice?

I was so upset I started to hyperventilate as I drove back to Cambridge and I threw up on my steering wheel. I was crying so much I couldn't breathe and I had to pull over to calm myself down. From that moment on, that car always reminded me of Dorset Girl and that night. It was only a matter of time before it had to go.

♥ DEAR OLLIE: GETTING OVER ♥ A BREAK-UP

If someone has broken up with you, there are a few things that it is very important to do:

- First, and most importantly, when it comes to the period after a break-up, it's time for you to be completely selfish and do anything you can to avoid being hurt further. I believe – and don't scream at me – that the only way you can begin to get over someone is by starting a (healthy) obsession with someone else.
- Then, if you can, go on holiday as soon as possible. Or at the very least take some time off work or uni to get your head around things. Go on a break to Cornwall, it worked for me!
- Avoid places that remind you of your ex. It's not always easy, I know. A smell, a song or a place will take you straight back to where you once were in a relationship, and there are always constant reminders. I always find Duty Free shops in airports fairly nostalgic, if not conducive to self-harming. You walk in to get a box of cigarettes, and before you know it you find yourself smelling the perfume your last love wore to remind yourself of the good times. Then you wind up sitting depressed all the way to South Africa.

If needs be, get someone else to buy your bargain vodka for you. Richard Dinan has had so many exes who have worn Viktor & Rolf's Flowerbomb perfume that he can't smell it without being reminded of several break-ups. I remember drunkenly spraying it all over Gabriella on the way back from that notorious Italy trip, so he had to smell it all the way home. Even now if he meets a girl who smells of it and he likes her, he has to think twice about asking her out because there is so much history in that scent.

- You have to delete your ex from your life. Remove them from Facebook, Twitter, Bebo, Myspace or any social networking site that could allow you to see photos of them enjoying themselves. To this day, even Gabriella is still pending as a friend on Facebook. It's now become a standing joke that I won't accept her. Imagine if you're following your ex on Twitter, and they start tweeting messages about how good last night was and tag some rugby player, or some hot blond you've never met before. It would make you think the worst, even if it's innocent. Why put yourself through that?

- Don't assume that just because your ex has moved on before you that they're the happy one. They may be uploading cosy pictures to Facebook but that doesn't mean they're over you. My friend Lucy Facebook-stalked her ex every hour after their break-up. She kept seeing him befriending different girls, who would write flirty messages on his wall, and she'd be devastated that he was having such a good time while she was still in the depths of despair. All she could think about was what he might be up to with those girls, but although he admitted that, yes, he was sleeping with other people, he was more unhappy than he'd ever been. He just wanted the company and, selfish as it was, he didn't give a shit about those girls. He needed someone to cuddle and help take his mind off Lucy.

- Speaking from personal experience, it also helps if you can avoid going out with people in the public eye. I once dated someone in the press, and when she started seeing someone else it was all over the *Mail* online. Thankfully I've got some lovely journalist friends who called me up beforehand to warn me but it would have been awful to find out via a website or magazine that my ex had officially moved on while I was still listening to Whitney on repeat after three bottles of red.

- This leads me on nicely to say never underestimate the importance of depressing songs when you're going through a break-up. I find Whitney, Celine Dion, James Blunt and Snow Patrol are all superior choices.

- You are allowed up to a month of serious crying, drinking too much and moaning to your friends. It's not until the last tear has been shed that you can get over that person, so let it all out. Then you need to start the healing process. No one wants to listen to you whining forever.

- Until you can go to bed at night and realise that you haven't thought about that person all day, you're not over them. So find someone else, anyone else, to focus on.

CHAPTER 11

INBETWEEN A HEARTBREAK AND THE COTSWOLDS

———

I returned to Cambridge a broken man. So I did what all normal people do and went and bought a rabbit, which I called Shakespeare. I spent the next four weeks watching *Great Expectations*, stroking my rabbit (that is *not* a euphemism) and crying into a bottle of very cheap red wine. It was like a scene from *Bridget Jones*, but worse. When my drama teacher told me I needed to see a shrink to get over my break-up I realised I wasn't doing a great job of hiding my heartache. I may have needed a psychiatrist but I didn't take her up on her advice. It was something I wanted to work through on my own.

We all fall in love, and if you haven't already then you certainly will at some point. Through the ages love has always been the same – complicated. *Pride and Prejudice* has now been swapped with *Bridget*

Jones, Shakespeare's *Taming of the Shrew* has become *10 Things I Hate About You*, and Jane Austin's *Emma* is now a fashion-obsessed American student in *Clueless*.

Love has been around since the beginning of time, and what I have realised at my tender age is that there are no rules, no guidelines and no simple way of sorting out the lessons that life seems to hand us when we're least expecting it.

If I could invent anything it would be a love pill that you take to magically make all of the hurt of a break-up melt away. I think if that existed people would be much braver and take more risks when it comes to love because they wouldn't have to worry about being hurt. And I would be a very rich man in the process!

I honestly think there was a time when I totally closed my heart to prevent getting hurt again. I felt like the pain of losing someone and the inevitable fallout wasn't worth it. It took me a long time to weigh it up and decide that maybe love is a risk worth taking after all.

Phase two of my 'getting over Dorset Girl' strategy involved me going out and getting drunk every night. I'd try to snog any girl I could in a bid to make myself feel better, and I managed to snog 32 girls in a single month. Sadly, if I remember rightly, none of them were particularly attractive.

One night I was in a club called Cindy's when I met a Polish cleaner who worked in a nearby hotel.

In my hammered state I decided that she was going to be my next girlfriend. She didn't seem that interested in me, so to make myself more appealing I lied and told her that I was in *EastEnders*. It worked, but the following morning I realised that we weren't a match made in sober heaven. Especially as she was allergic to rabbit hair and had to leave before we could consummate our newly found friendship.

About six weeks after my split from Dorset Girl I finally felt I was on the right path to getting over her when she called to tell me that her period was eight weeks late. In a state of panic, I immediately drove down to see her and to be with her while she did a pregnancy test. Fortunately it was a false alarm as her period came that afternoon. She seemed to need closure and the break-up had put her body out of sync, but seeing her again had set me right back and I missed her more than ever. So I headed back to Cambridge to drink more wine.

We were invited to go and look around the RADA building in London and to see some of the third-year students' plays. On the journey we were all larking about and we started talking about how we lost our virginity. I hadn't thought about Jesters Girl for some time, so I decided to phone her out of the blue. As luck would have it, she was in London with her friend, London Girl.

I'd always got on well with London Girl. When I used to give Jesters Girl the dodgy driving lessons around Ascot in my Fiesta, she'd always come along and sit in the back. I'd often have a bag of Haribo sweets in my car and I remember once looking into the rear-view mirror to see her putting the Haribo rings on each of her fingers and sucking them off innocently, one by one.

I couldn't take my eyes off her, which isn't the safest thing when you're driving. I thought to myself, 'I think I fancy her.' Not the best thought to have when you're dating her best friend.

With that sexy memory still fresh in my mind, I arranged to meet them. Jesters Girl had to rush off, so London Girl and I decided to hang out. It was a Friday evening and we were both in the mood for having a few drinks and some fun. London Girl was as stunning as I remembered her – 5 foot 9, slim, with beautiful red hair. We had a great evening and ended up back at her place, watching a film in bed. One of the characters in the movie said, 'I hate it when you really like someone and they won't make a move,' at which point London Girl looked at me and said, 'Yes, I hate it when that happens.' To this day, she will always deny that she used that line to try to make me kiss her. But I knew differently and I took that as a hint, and I'm glad I did. I rolled over and kissed her and we spent the next five hours laughing, smiling and kissing. For the first time in months, I felt genuinely happy.

But life is never that easy – the next day London Girl left to go travelling for five months, so I wasn't sure if we had any kind of future. We kissed goodbye and promised to keep in touch.

It was the final few weeks of my course at Cambridge and I'd agreed to model in a friend's end-of-term fashion show. I'd been to fashion shows before and seen all of the models drinking backstage, so I assumed it was the done thing and that if I were to be a proper model I should do it too. I went to the shop and bought a quarter bottle of vodka and downed the whole thing. Unsurprisingly, I was obliterated. My friends even tried to stop me going on stage because I was so pissed, but I managed to convince them I was OK. I got my best model face on, way too much fake tan, and prepared for the runway. I had spiked my hair up and made it massive. In my mind I looked like Ryan Gosling with a bigger barnet, but in reality I looked like *Zoolander*'s Sri Lankan cousin.

I strutted my stuff down the catwalk, my confidence boosted by the alcohol. I felt like I was oozing attitude and professionalism so I decided to light a cigarette on the way, thinking it would look really cool. I looked like a complete twat.

We all went to a bar afterwards to celebrate the show, which despite my best efforts had gone tremendously well.

I had a couple more drinks before stumbling to the toilet, where I promptly fell asleep in a cubicle. My friend Adam found me, picked me up and carried me upstairs to our table, where I unceremoniously vomited all over it, right in front of some of the most beautiful and eligible girls on my course. That marked the end of my time at Cambridge. Unsurprisingly, I was ready to move on and to focus all my energies on acting.

I'd applied to a number of drama schools with a view to doing a drama degree, and I was excited about putting everything I'd learned at Cambridge into practice.

I got that opportunity when I heard about an audition for a new TV show. The production company was looking for a young posh guy. 'Perfect,' I thought. 'I'm young, I'm posh and I'm about to leave drama school. I can do it.' I emailed them pretending that I was a Cambridge University student imaginatively named Jerry Horowitz and was duly invited to an audition in London.

After making the journey to a random building in central London they gave me the script but promptly told me that they couldn't pinpoint which character I could be. Not a great sign. I carried on with the audition regardless, but to be honest I was quite nervous and a bit shit. It's just that I wanted it so badly. I had to act out a scene where four boys go to an off-licence to try and buy Drambuie. It was funny to watch that same scene sometime later on a show you may have heard of called *The Inbetweeners*. Needless to say, I didn't get the part of Will.

When term finished I decided to go travelling around India for a month with seven female friends. I felt like I needed to totally get away from everything.

We rode camels and had amazing parties and slept under the stars in the desert or in very scummy hotels, and I had a lot of time to think about what I wanted to do with my life. All that kept popping into my head was acting, so I knew I'd done the right thing applying for some drama schools before I left England. I decided to focus all of my energy on performing and let love take a back seat for a while, so when I arrived home and received the letters that said my application hadn't been successful, I was devastated.

Acting had been my plan for 10 years and I wasn't particularly good at or interested in anything else. I felt totally and utterly lost. In the end, I did something that no one expected, including myself: I enrolled in an agricultural university so I could learn how to be a farmer.

OK, so I know what you're thinking: Ollie Locke at farmers' college? That never happened. But I promise you, that's what happened! I was accepted onto a course at the Royal Agricultural College in Cirencester to study Property Agency and Marketing. It was a last-minute panicked decision, and one that I would live to regret (ish).

Now, you know me, I like to stand out, so I decided that as I was starting university I didn't really want to conform to the stereotypical countryside dress code. I needed a makeover. So I started calling myself Lockey, and adopted a slightly edgy look.

My reinvention began with a very painful tongue piercing, which involved an ugly, bearded man putting his fingers in my mouth and sticking a needle though my tongue, which duly swelled up so much it resembled a side of beef. I also bought a pair of vintage cowboy boots and 12 pairs of white jeans to complete my look. What more could I need for a degree in property? I was all set for my new adventure.

Now, as you may have already noticed, things rarely go to plan when I'm involved, and sure enough upon arrival at Cirencester I discovered that my details had somehow got lost and there was no place for me in the halls of residence. Instead, I was given a room in a house away from the town, with four men who hardly spoke a word of English. It wasn't ideal, and to make matters worse they didn't seem to understand what not pissing on the toilet seat meant.

While everyone in halls was having a jolly old time, with parties every night and getting to know each other, I was stuck off campus with a bunch of men who'd pass me in the kitchen without so much as a 'hello'. It was so miserable.

The only saving grace was that the house itself was incredible. It had a big open fire, a grand piano and a drinks cabinet in my bedroom, and it only cost £86 a week. There were horses to ride, shooting rights in case I fancied giving it a go, and a swimming pool. I definitely did university in style.

It's all changed now, but back in the day Cirencester was the kind of university where after dinner women would go into one room and guys would go into another. I'm not exaggerating when I say the men would wear smoking jackets and drink expensive whisky as if they were in *Downton Abbey*. It was *beyond* posh. My Fiesta was by far the shittest car there, besides a couple of old tractors, and it didn't have any hunting or shooting stickers on the back so it stood out a mile.

My fresher's initiation at Cirencester involved drinking wee and sick from a pint glass with squirty cream and a flake on top. I drank about a quarter of a pint before I threw up violently, so I failed the first hurdle to becoming one of the lads.

No matter how hard I tried, I just didn't fit in. I had long hair and a tongue piercing and I was into fashion. I remember finally getting an invite to one of the other guy's country houses for a party and during a game of truth or dare I admitted that I'd once snogged a man. Nobody in that group spoke to me normally again after that day, and I was never invited to another party. I was effectively ostracised.

I had one really great friend called Guy, who was the only person who really stood by me. He was proper country and even owned a partridge farm in

Norfolk, but he was very loyal to me and I thought he was a lovely guy.

I was so unhappy that I only went to 14 lectures in the whole of my first year. The only light on the horizon was London Girl, who had returned from travelling at the start of the university year. That brief night of passion had left a lasting impression so I was thrilled when she got back in touch upon her return. Tanned and glowing from her travels, she was every bit as stunning as I remembered. And she was my girlfriend.

CHAPTER 12

LONDON CALLING

———

London Girl was studying in Oxford and before long we'd started a long-distance relationship. It was hard to find myself in that situation again, saying goodbye week after week as I had done with Dorset Girl, but I knew that London Girl was special.

We hadn't told Jesters Girl that we were seeing each other yet because we were both a bit worried about how she would react. It's never fun when your friend dates your ex. But in the end, of course, we had to tell her and Jesters Girl was lovely about it.

I had really become quite besotted with London Girl; they say love makes you do strange things, which must account for what I did next. I had started to get panicked by the thought of thousands of good-looking rugby playing freshers at her uni, all full of sperm, all pumped up on vodka and Red Bull, trying it on with her. Not that I didn't trust her, but I certainly didn't trust them. So to ease my mind I ordered a full-size cardboard cutout of myself so it could stand at the end of her bed. That way any guy who dared to enter her room with unsavoury intentions would be faced with my glaring, disapproving face.

I got it made in my hometown of Southampton and it cost me £120. It looked amazing, but there was the small problem of getting it to her. My car had broken down and I was due to visit her, so I decided to get the train from Southampton to London and then on to Oxford.

Because it was life-size the rail company made me pay for a seat for it, so that set me back another £20. I think she was quite shocked when I showed up with it. I'd told her I was bringing her a special present and I think she was expecting jewellery.

I felt like it would guilt her into staying faithful when all those horny uni boys were flocking round her. Remember, I was a guy, and I knew the kind of thoughts they had.

I have never, ever cheated on a girlfriend, and I never would. I feel so guilty about everything anyway that I don't have it in me. I don't know if anyone has ever cheated on me – apart from one girlfriend a short while ago and Tilly, sort of. (Even though we were never properly together I felt that way whenever she left me to go to her actual boyfriend.)

If other girls have cheated, I don't want to know. It's better to finish the relationship without me knowing. Ignorance is bliss. Why would I need that information now? It won't change anything and all it would do is make me more paranoid in future relationships and hurt a lot more.

If I did find out a girl was cheating on me while we were in a serious relationship, that would be it. It would be over; there would be no second chances. I would advise any friend of mine to do the same. It's so disrespectful and it ruins people's sense of trust, which is so selfish.

I know a guy who is 55 and someone he was in love with when he was 20 cheated on him; he has never been able to regain a sense of trust, so he has never got into a relationship again. It's scarred him for life and I think it's the worst thing you can do to someone you care for. If you are thinking about doing it, don't. It's not worth it for a bit of fun. And if it's more than a bit of fun, that's even worse. If you don't want to be with someone then split up with them and give them a chance to meet someone else. Don't leave them hanging around because you're too scared to break the bad news to them, *especially* if it's because you like someone else.

It's just so sad when one bad relationship changes people's views forever, and if someone ever cheats on you, no matter how much you love them, in my opinion you will never be able to trust them again, so you're better off out of the relationship.

For some reason men always get a bad deal when it comes to cheating as everyone assumes they're much worse than women. I know for a fact that one of my best friends, Barnaby, once slept with four married women in a single week.

He pulled a girl in a club one night and they ended up back at his house. The next morning she turned round to him without a hint of irony and said, 'Have you got any perfume? I'm seeing my husband for lunch and I want to smell nice.'

Barnaby and I lived with another guy, Alex, for a while (more on both of them later) and Alex and I had this ritual where, if we were both free, we'd go to Ikea on a Tuesday and have meatballs for dinner. It's a guilty pleasure. I liked going to one particular branch because there was a girl who worked there who was unbelievably beautiful.

We were there one night tucking into our meatballs when Barnaby texted us to say that he was stuck in our kitchen. As the story unfolded we discovered that he had been having sex with a girl on the kitchen worksurface, and when he'd turned the handle on the door to get out, it had come off in his hand. We raced back to let him out, and when we eventually managed to open the door we found them both standing there, stark naked. Obviously we found the whole thing hysterical, while they ran down the hall-way to get clothes.

Barnaby found it quite amusing, but his partner in crime didn't and she threw a massive shit fit when she realised how late it was. Her reason? She was supposed to be having dinner with her fiancé that night!

Anyway, back to the story. It was about four months into my relationship with London Girl and I thought things were going brilliantly. She was due to visit, so I persuaded Guy to come with me when I went to pick her up from the station. When I went to introduce them, everything went really quiet and it soon became clear that they already knew each other. They'd been shagging for a couple of months the previous summer, before London Girl and I had got together. My two main insecurities back then were people who were taller or better-looking than me, and Guy was both. They met each other when they went stalking deer together in Scotland with their respective families.

They were both completely mortified and we tried to talk about it that night but it was so weird. It wasn't like they had cheated on me. Neither of them had even known me then. But it was a shit, shit situation.

Even though it wasn't Guy's fault at all I barely spoke to him for the next couple of weeks. He even sent me flowers to say sorry, but there was nothing either of them could do to make me feel better. I felt so hurt by it, even though I knew I was being irrational.

By the end of the first year, I had come to accept that Cirencester was totally wrong for me. I didn't fit in. I didn't wear a Barbour jacket 24 hours a day or go hunting, for which I used to get bullied. People would piss on the door handles of my car.

I was so happy when June rolled around and it was time to leave. I knew there was no way I would be going back for the second year, so I dropped out, despite having no idea what I was going to do next. For some reason I wasn't at all worried. I knew that everything would be OK.

I didn't want to go back to living in Southampton and I wasn't in a position to move up to London, so I decided to pretty much move in with London Girl in her halls in Oxford. I'd got over the whole thing with Guy, and our relationship was stronger than ever. London Girl was the first person I said 'I love you' to. We were lying together in her single bed at halls, and just as we were falling asleep she turned to me and said, 'I love you.' Like me, she'd never said it to anyone before so it was a big deal for her, and I did have to think briefly about whether or not to say it back. But actually, it felt right.

I sometimes worry that I'll never get that incredible feeling again with anyone. I've had relationships since but nothing has evoked that same feeling of

Brent Library Service

Customer ID: *******3425

Items that you have renewed

Title: Laid in Chelsea : my life
uncovered
ID: 91120000114751
Due: **30 April 2020**

Total items: 1
Account balance: £0.15
19/03/2020 17:04
Borrowed: 1
Overdue: 0
Hold requests: 0
Ready for collection: 0

total contentment and happiness. Maybe it's something to do with being young and as you get older that emotional high wanes. Who knows? Maybe we are more realistic now. I'm definitely on my guard more than I used to be, and I'm more wary of jumping into things. I guess when you're young you don't worry as much about being hurt or things going wrong.

Looking back, we were besotted with one another. One of my favourite memories is of waking up in bed with London Girl at her mum's house in London with the sun streaming through the windows. It was so cosy and romantic and I can still take myself back to that moment in a second. We used to travel to London as often as we could because we both loved going out exploring together. I fell more in love with London Girl and with London with each visit.

A not-so-happy memory is another Valentine's Day disaster. See? I told you that day is a total nightmare.

I'd booked London Girl and myself a junior suite at The Ritz. I was determined that, for once, Valentine's Day would be perfect. After my Paris disaster I was ready to give up on the whole thing but the romantic in me still wanted to believe that it could all be wonderful.

Now, I had never taken Viagra before, but a friend of mine gave me one so I decided to give it a go that night. Much to my disappointment it didn't work, and by then the moment had been ruined, so after all of that build-up London Girl and I ended up having an early night after some supper. At least I didn't get the shits this time.

We moved past that quite literal let down and had just celebrated our two-year anniversary when Christian, a friend of mine from Cambridge, called to invite me onto his boat for Cowes Week.

Cowes Week is the world's biggest sailing regatta, and I've been every year since I was young. I've inherited my love of sailing from my dad, who was once a big sailor and came third in the world championships of the 505 yacht class in the 1970s. It's a fabulous week of parties and sailing; the champagne and conversation flows, while wealthy yacht owners and enthusiasts watch the races. The first evening, I met a beautiful girl called Antalya Nall-Cain, who is the daughter of Lord Brocket (who you may know following his appearance on *I'm a Celebrity … Get Me Out of Here!*). Antalya and I hit it off straight away, but purely on a platonic level.

Antalya wouldn't stop talking about this guy she was seeing. She said he was very posh and lived on a grand estate in the middle of Buckinghamshire, and that I would love him. I wasn't so sure. The idea of having to spend the next five days on a boat with someone who sounded almost identical to the pricks

I went to uni with sounded horrendous. But I wasn't going to judge him before I'd even met him.

Later that evening a small dingy boasting a Union Jack flag made its way to the boat where we were staying. Suddenly a blond Hugh Grant type tripped onto the boat with a huge smile and a bottle of champagne in his hand. That was the moment Antalya's boyfriend, Richard Dinan, entered my life. I knew from the grin on his face and the fact that he tripped up the stairs, and dropped the champagne that this was a man I would like.

We all sat down with candles and wine, overlooking the ocean, to eat the mackerel I had caught earlier in the day. Slowly everyone went back to their cabins to sleep, but I stayed outside drinking wine and writing, which are two of my favourite things in the world.

Richard came out to join me because he couldn't sleep, and we spent hours talking and watching the sunrise. He asked me what I wanted to do now I had finished university. I told him that I had absolutely no idea. He explained that he owned a small magazine and asked if I wanted to go and work for him. Even though I'm dyslexic I have a real passion for writing and I've always kept journals and written short stories. It sounded perfect. So, partly due to an excitable wine haze, I accepted the job there and then.

Cowes Week ended but a new chapter and a new friendship in my life began.

London Girl came to join us the next day and when I told her my news she was happy for me but I think she was also a bit worried about what would become of us. I assured her that we could survive anything, and I truly believed it. I told her I loved her. And I did. And that was all that mattered.

♥ DEAR OLLIE: SAYING ♥ 'I LOVE YOU'

Telling someone you love them can be incredibly dangerous and potentially hurtful, simply because you don't know if they're going to say it back and you might end up looking like a knob. If they do, that's wonderful. If they don't, they are clearly very far away from being ready to say those three all-important words, but you can't see it. You have to be pretty certain someone is going to say it back before you dive in head first.

No matter how smitten you are, never say the 'L' word before you've been going out for at least three months. You're in a delusional honeymoon period and you're not thinking straight. I was once so in love with London Girl that I wrote her the craziest email, of which I still have a copy today. It read: 'This feeling of positioned dedication and understanding ... How can any feeling relate to a certain grasp of emotion. Love is a power. Love is a grasp. A fist clenched tight to ensure nothing comes loose. Not only in the heart, but in every vein and every bone and every sense of the body. Until broken the heart only acts as a mechanism, pushing it harder, deeper, into undiscovered places. Although uncertain of the future, it only matters what happens in the present. Taking every day as its last, as if every kiss was a silent theme tune, every close moment is followed by a sepia video, and every word is recorded and kept in a montage of distant memories, only remembered by a song, a ballet, a street artist, or that unsure relation to a timeless connection.'

I read that back now and I think, 'What the fuck was I writing?' But at the time I was in some kind of love trance. When you're first falling for someone you feel such deep, empowering love you don't know what you're doing. I would never write something like that now and I can laugh at it, but that's the effect that love had on me.

Before you can really say 'I love you' and mean it 100 per cent you must be certain that what you feel is real. Therefore I recommend that you follow these three steps to building up to those three little words.

1. Start by saying 'love ya', which can be said flippantly over the phone or in a text and suggests that things are still much more on a good friendship level.
2. Next move to 'love you', which gently eases you into the big reveal.
3. You add in the big 'I'. In some ways, this little vowel is the most important, and until you can say those three words together, you're not at that stage where you can totally commit to someone.

There is nothing worse than saying 'I love you' by mistake. When you're cuddling up on the sofa with someone and they say something funny and without realising it you've laughed and said, 'Ahhh, I love you!' Once it's out there you can't take it back. It's like the humiliation and awkwardness of calling your teacher 'mum' when you're at school, but amplified by a million.

If you then turn around and say you didn't mean it and you don't love them, it only makes things worse and sets the relationship back months.

I went out with one girl in my mid-20s and we told each other we loved each other within a month. Looking back I can see that there's a very thin line between infatuation and love. There are times when you want to be with someone 24 hours a day because you're almost addicted to them. But you can't sustain that initial intensity and the relationship will ultimately fail. I realised after a couple of months that actually, I didn't love her, so those precious words felt false.

When it comes to saying 'I love you', I don't believe you should ever play games. There are people who won't say it back to someone just so they have the upper hand. If you love somebody, let them know. Just choose your time wisely and make sure you really, really mean it.

I came up with an equation while writing this book that I like to call 'The Ollie Locke theory of relationship success'.

With love, the only time you are really 100 per cent happy is at the moment you kiss on your wedding day. After that, it's a free-for-all, open to all the elements of life. You need your happiness percentage to rise and fall to keep a relationship happy and healthy, and if both parties follow these rules carefully, you should be in a good position to have a happy relationship. It's very simple.

So, you are both feeling amazing and life is going well, you got married three months ago and you recently returned from your honeymoon. You get promoted at work and you're cruising along at 74 per cent happy. Your partner is at a stable 60 per cent; they aren't as happy because work is going badly. They then get a phone call to say their family dog died, which puts them at 42 per cent happy. When they subsequently lose their job, their happiness level dramatically falls to 19 per cent. Your happiness then falls to 45 per cent as you begin to worry about bills and how you're going to support everything on your own. It is at this point you should recognise your partner's need for love and attention and do something lovely for them to boost their happiness level. A surprise dinner at their favourite restaurant followed by a candlelit bath boosts their love for you and their level rises to a healthier 32 per cent. In the meantime, you have been treated to an evening of sex so your level rises to 51 per cent. Then a week later your partner gets offered their dream job in television and their happiness level rises to 60 per cent while you, no longer worried about finances, go back up to 68 per cent. Even the smallest of elements could change your percentage on a minute-by-minute basis, from being stuck in a traffic jam to the photocopier at work breaking down, to being starving and finding the shop has sold out of your favourite bagel. The simplest of things will make a change, and your percentage is constantly on the move.

But the main point of this is for you to recognise how your other half is feeling and what they are currently going though in *their* life, putting yours on the back burner. Sometimes all you need is a small gesture like a bunch of flowers to show your love and support.

Both of you are always working towards 100, but you never actually want to get there, because after too long at 100 per cent things will start to get boring. It's too safe, it's too smooth. Love feeds on the fight between people, the differences you share and your ability to work together as a union. Only then can you be truly happy in a relationship.

CHAPTER 13

RACHEL STEVENS AND MOPPING UP VOMIT (NOT HERS)

So the future was looking bright. I returned from Cowes to Southampton, excitedly packed a suitcase and moved to Beaconsfield, where Richard was based. I stayed with his parents and planned to move to London as soon as possible and commute down to work on the magazine.

I had a wonderful time living with Richard's family. Their house is beautiful, and Richard and I used to drink brandy and sing *Phantom of the Opera* at the top of our voices. We'd make up songs together and Richard would play the piano while I sang along. We were like an old gay married couple living in the 1920s – with no sex, obviously. I loved working for his magazine – I was writing and that's what I wanted to do. It wasn't a paid job, so it wasn't a long-term prospect, but I got to go to photo shoots and to interview designers and I loved it. After a couple of months, it was time for me to move on and earn some money and get my own place. I promised myself that I would go back to writing one day, but I put down the laptop and started a new chapter in my life. A friend from my Cambridge drama course, Gabby, phoned to say she knew of a place in Swiss Cottage, North London, where we could stay for free. The only condition was that we had to be in by 8pm every evening. We were basically house-sitting to prevent squatters living there, so someone had to be in the flat every night to make sure no unsavoury types tried to break in.

It sounded perfect. I packed my things and headed for London – my dream to move to the Big Smoke was a reality at last.

There was just one problem – Gabby had neglected to tell me that there was no furniture whatsoever in the house. There wasn't even a knife and fork. I had to sleep on a World War II stretcher that I found in the shed, which was covered in blood stains – I struggle to think how I could have been any more uncomfortable or unhygienic.

Gabby had a very unusual occupation: she was a working clown. I used to get woken up by her giant squeaking shoes every morning after about two hours of sleep, so it didn't quite turn out to be the paradise I was dreaming of. London Girl couldn't even come and stay because there was nowhere for her to sleep, and unsurprisingly the blood-stained stretcher didn't appeal.

Before long I had no money and I began to wonder if moving to London had been the right thing to do after all. Then Gabby came home and announced, while still wearing her clown outfit, that we were moving to Belgrave Square to house-sit another vacant property.

Belgrave Square is one of the most exclusive addresses in London, and for the very first time I was going to be living in Chelsea.

I threw myself into Chelsea life, and Richard and I started going to a club called 151 on the King's Road practically every night. It's known as 'The Dive' because it is one, but fabulous people go there because no one expects them to, so there are never any paps outside. It is by far my favourite club in London.

Over the years I went there, celebrities would come in and out and you would see wealthy middle-aged bankers buying drinks for hot Sloaney 21-year-olds, the outline of their wedding rings still visible through their shirt top pockets. The club housed some of the most beautiful women in London, because they all wanted somewhere they could go to dance to cheesy music. There was a big group of us who became regulars, and we got on well with the staff and particularly Rollo, the bar manager. It was like having a second home because I could walk in at any time and I'd know everyone there (even now, I walk in, go behind the bar and pour myself a drink). After not fitting in to university life in Cirencester, it was a welcome relief. I was 20 years old, with no responsibilities, and I was making the most of it.

Seeing as I was spending so much time there, it made sense for me to start working at 151 in the evenings to earn some extra money, basically doing whatever they needed me to. I even DJ'd one night when the regular guy didn't turn up. I had no idea what I was doing as I tried to mix these CDs together. It was ridiculous.

My new job at 151 wound London Girl up a lot because I was spending more and more time in London, and less time with her. Not to mention the fact that I had hot blondes all around me. I was hanging out with Richard all the time, as well as new friends Freddie Van Zevenbergen and George Askew. George had been the first ever public schoolboy to go into *Big Brother* a couple of months earlier. He promptly walked out after just 13 days and had become notorious as a result.

One evening, Freddie suggested that we all go to a cool place called the Cuckoo Club. The club was having an anniversary and Halloween party, and it sounded like it was going to be an amazing night.

We all met outside and Freddie turned up with a Moët cool bag. He unzipped it to reveal a live lobster inside. I asked him why the hell he had it and he replied, 'Well, the theme is a touch of purple, so I brought Monty along.' It sounds weird because everyone knows that lobsters are orange, but they have a purple hue before they're cooked. He even had a little diamanté lead for the lobster, which until that night had been living in a tank at his house.

About halfway through the evening Freddie said he was getting a bit tired of holding Monty, and that he was going to drop him off. We presumed he was putting him back in the cool bag, but about 20 minutes later a waiter rolled up with Monty on a plate, cooked. Neither of us could believe it but we were also very hungry. Yes, I'm ashamed to say, we all sat there and ate Monty. It was so dark, but delicious.

People always ask me why I have such an obsession with the Union Jack and why I'm so patriotic. My answer is always the same – that it began one night back in 2007.

Tatler magazine had interviewed Richard about being a young entrepreneur. We were all invited to *Tatler*'s Little Black Book party, which was basically a list of 100 of London society's most eligible bachelors and bacheloresses. George's mum Rosemary – who was private secretary to Prince Charles for many years – offered us a lift. We all got dressed up and climbed into her vintage open-topped Aston Martin. She put on the James Bond theme and we drove down The

Mall with hundreds of Union Jacks lining the streets. It's still one of my favourite moments of living in London and sometimes even now I take a detour to drive my own Union Jack Jaguar down The Mall, just to feel really British.

When we arrived the paps went a bit crazy for George but no one knew who I was: I was a nobody. A photographer asked me, George and Richard if he could take a photo, but then pushed me out of the way and said, 'No, not you.' I have never felt so small. But that dick photographer didn't dampen my love of the London party scene – nor was it the last time I saw him.

Around this time, Rachel Stevens crossed my path again. Yes, if I hadn't made a total idiot of myself during our first encounter, I definitely did the second time we met.

It was at an after-party at The Old Vic theatre. I'd been to watch a 24-hour play, where loads of amazing actors have 24 hours to improvise a play. It was absolutely incredible. Across the crowded room, I spotted Rachel Stevens, who was looking as beautiful as ever. I was so sure she would remember me – it had only been a few years since we'd spent that special time together, so how could she not? Shyness masked by the couple of glasses of champagne I had drunk, I marched right over to her, exclaiming, 'You'll never believe what happened, Tululla got expelled!' She looked at me with a massive 'who the fuck are you?'

look on her face. Undeterred, I carried on rambling, even introducing her to my sister. I have to give Rachel credit, she was absolutely delightful and acted as if she knew exactly who I was, which was so sweet of her. You'd think I would have learned from my experience with Hattie Clark! I just hope that if I do ever meet Rachel again, it'll be third time lucky.

My fabulous life in London continued to cause not so fabulous problems between London Girl and me. While I was totally faithful, my world had completely changed, and our lives were going in different directions.

I loved living in London and I loved my job at 151, even if it did involve clearing up sick or carrying people out to chauffeur-driven cars. As harsh as it sounds, there simply wasn't as much room as there should have been for London Girl.

Something had shifted between us and I didn't feel like I used to. I still loved her enormously, but I knew I couldn't be with her any more.

Not long before we went our separate ways, we went on holiday with Jesters Girl and her family to Portugal. I've got a photo that was taken of us on the beach that week. Looking back at it now I realise that it was at that exact moment I knew 100 per cent that we had to split up. I have no idea why, something just clicked inside of me and that was it.

She looks amazing in the picture. Everything I loved her for is shining through, whereas I'm looking uncomfortable and emotionless because I knew, whether I wanted it or not, it was the end for us.

London Girl and I had become so comfortable with each other and we relied on each other so much that the thought of breaking up made me incredibly sad. But I knew it was for the best, although neither of us wanted to admit it to ourselves, or each other.

We managed to make it through the rest of the holiday, trying to enjoy it as much as we could. London Girl knew something was wrong so she kept making even more of an effort, which just made things worse.

We flew back home and headed to her mum's house in London. We went to bed and just as I was about to fall asleep, I heard her say, 'I know you've got something to tell me.' I knew my reply immediately but I froze and thought about the last three years and how I was about to lose everything. 'Yes, I want us to break up,' I replied. She burst into tears – although about five minutes later the tables flipped as I turned into a blabbering child and she had to spend the next three hours comforting me.

As selfish as it sounds and as much as I did love London Girl, I knew I needed to be on my own, living my new life in London. I had something to get out of my system, and three years is a hell of a long time to be in a relationship at that age. At the time it seemed silly not to give myself a chance to really enjoy myself while I had so much opportunity to do so. It was a decision that I would regret later on down the line.

The next day I left London Girl's house feeling something I'd never felt before – completely and utterly empty.

We gave each other as much space as we could for the next couple of weeks. I would hear through her friends about how she was doing, and I had to resist the temptation to jump on the bus to Oxford whenever I saw one drive down the streets around Victoria Station.

A month had passed when on one Sunday afternoon London Girl arrived on my doorstep. We both broke down in tears and held each other tightly. I was scared that if I let go I'd never see her again, but after sitting and talking for hours, I knew I had to let her go for good.

I'll never forget her leaving that final time. I hailed her a black cab, and as it drove off I chased the taxi down the road, knowing it might be the last I ever saw of her. It was completely and utterly heartbreaking. This may sound like a scene from a cheesy romcom but that's the way it happened, and as I stood there in the middle of the road with tears streaming down my face, I wished I could rewind to the amazing times we had when we first got together.

I spent the next day sitting on the wall outside the Royal Court Theatre. I watched the world turn around me because it was all I could do; I was numb. The person I loved more than anyone else in the world was no longer in my life. I didn't know what to think or feel. She was gone and that chapter was over.

♥ DEAR OLLIE: BREAKING UP ♥ WITH SOMEONE

Is there ever a good way to break up with someone? In short, no, but there are some good ways to make the break-up better for everyone involved:

1. Do it on neutral ground but not in public and not somewhere the person you're splitting up with is going to have to go regularly.
2. Avoid doing it over the phone because you owe them the respect of having a face-to-face conversation – unless they've cheated on you, in which case a text will suffice.
3. Never say 'it's not you, it's me' because it's the world's biggest cliché and no one appreciates it. Even if this is the case, reword that awful line to make it sound like you've at least thought about what you were going to say.
4. Be totally upfront, and if you've fallen out of love with someone, be honest and tell them. It may seem incredibly harsh but it will help both of you to move on more quickly.
5. Don't get pissed before you do it because no matter how carefully you plan your words, they will no doubt end up coming out wrong.

6. If they cry, hug them and be there for them – if they want you to, of course. They may decide they never want to see you again, but give them the option.

7. Do not do it within a month of Christmas, their birthday, Valentine's Day, or the anniversary of their dog's death. You may be dumping them but you don't want to seem like a complete arsehole.

8. Never do it when they're about to go on holiday – wait until they are back. Selfish as it sounds, you'll only be giving yourself a really shit two weeks as they'll inevitably be on a shagging rampage in the Swiss Alps.

9. Never do it in their bed. I did that to both London Girl and Gabriella – I really need to learn from my mistake. You have to think about what is best for the other person. At the end of the day, you were together because you cared about them, and just because you don't fancy or love them any more it doesn't mean you shouldn't treat them in the best way possible. You need to respect the time you spent together.

CHAPTER 14

A FUR COAT AND A COLONIC

When a relationship that means a lot to you comes to an end, it's hard to imagine that the pain will ever go away, but life, as they say, moves on, and so it was with London Girl and me. It was my toughest break-up yet and followed my longest relationship, so I planned to stay single for a while. It's said that you need six months to get over every year of a relationship, so I wanted to give myself space to adapt to being on my own.

They always say when you're not looking for it, romance finds you, and I must have been releasing some sort of pheromone – maybe one that said 'Yes, I'm single' – because I kept getting lots of attention, both female *and* male.

That time felt like my proper bachelor days. Not that I wanted to go out sleeping with loads of people or having one-night stands – my conscience would never let me. And I started to realise that there are amazing perks to being single. You're your own boss and you don't have to answer to anyone. That feeling of independence is incredible. Having said all of that, the sad thing is that I'm pretty shit at being on my own and, given the choice, I would always rather be in a relationship.

After breaking up with London Girl I decided I couldn't carry on house-sitting and that I needed a real base. I'd stayed in touch with Antalya – who by this point had split from Richard – and she introduced me to her brother Alex. Just like Antalya, Alex and I hit it off straight away and he is now one of my best friends in the world. Before long I'd moved in with him along with two other guys, Barnaby, who I've mentioned before, and Toby.

Living with them was like getting a crash course in being a lad, which I think it's quite clear I have never been. They are all very eligible in their own ways, and they absolutely love women, so we had a constant stream of girls coming in and out of the house.

I, on the other hand, ended up becoming the friendly housemate who would cook them breakfast the morning after, rather than the one shagging them. The funny thing is that since appearing on *Made in Chelsea*, I'm the one who gets most of the attention, but the guys will always try to swoop in and grab the girl. One of my friends even tells girls that he's starring in the next series just so he can increase his chances of pulling them. It's shocking, but it does work. Especially in Guildford. (Doesn't it, Barnaby?)

Even though the house itself was lovely, we were pretty disgusting. Alex has OCD and is very clean but the rest of us were the same as any guys in their early 20s. We rarely cleaned up after ourselves and would only empty the bin if our life depended on it, which didn't help poor Alex's obsession with cleanliness. I'm very house-proud and could think of nothing worse than having a dirty kitchen or bathroom now, but I have no idea how we managed to get any girls back to the place at all in those days.

I'll never forget the time we watched an episode of *Dirty Sanchez*, the Welsh version of *Jackass*. They were doing self-administered colonic irrigation and Barnaby decided it would be hilarious if he did the same using a piece of garden hose and an empty Coke bottle. I'll spare you the details, but it ended up with a big mess, me and Alex throwing up and Barnaby not being in any fit state to go on the date he had arranged for that evening as he was break-dancing in his own faeces.

We'd relentlessly pull pranks on each other. If anyone ever brought a girl back and was clearly having sex, Alex would play 'The Lion Sleeps Tonight' on his laptop on repeat and leave it outside their bedroom door. Even though I wasn't on the receiving end because I only ever brought two girlfriends to the house, I decided that it was time for him to have a taste of his own medicine, so I played 'The Wedding March' outside his room when he brought back a girl he'd liked for ages. Revenge was sweet.

It was all quite juvenile, but good fun. I would love to go back to those times because although thinking about sharing a house with those three reprobates makes me feel slightly sick, they provided me with some of my funniest memories of London.

London Girl made *another* brief reappearance while I was living with the guys. One Friday night I was having drinks with a friend when I noticed that London Girl had checked in at 151 on Facebook. I sat there mulling things over, knowing that I still loved her. My head was telling me no, but my heart does what it wants, and within 20 minutes I was running down the King's Road to the club. As soon as I saw her across the room dancing with friends, I forgot all the bad things about the relationship and I realised that I still missed her and loved her so much. I remember her double taking in shock as I walked in, and it felt amazing to hold her in my arms again.

We spent the night together, but the following day we ended up arguing about something irrelevant and she left with barely a goodbye. Suddenly everything felt really, really shit again.

I walked around the flat praying that one of the other boys was in so I could talk to someone. I was tired, hungover and I felt a real sense of despair about everything. When I realised I was alone, I burst into tears and slumped onto the floor, where I stayed for a few hours. I felt lonely, directionless and scared about the future. My hopes of becoming an actor were fading, I was all over the place when it came to London Girl and I knew that I couldn't spend the next few years of my life watching people throw up in clubs.

I pulled myself together for long enough to pack a bag and get to the number 211 bus to Waterloo station so I could go home to Southampton.

I took time off work and stayed for two weeks with my mum, drinking wine and talking about life. By the time I was ready to go back to London I felt like a weight had been lifted.

And, although I couldn't see it then, my life was about to take an unusual turn.

I felt it was time for me to move forward and get back on the dating scene – and the first person I got together with after London Girl was a man. Through mutual friends, I came to know a fantastic guy called James, who's gay, an artist and in his fifties. The first night I met him I knew that he was going to become a very close friend, and he's now one of my closest confidants. We had such a connection. But before you fast forward, he's not the guy I ended up with.

We'd been hanging out for a while when one day, out of the blue, James asked me, 'Ollie, have you ever done anything with a guy?' I said I found some men attractive, and had once kissed a man, but I didn't think I was gay. He smiled and said, 'Come to a dinner party with me next week.'

I wasn't sure if men were on the agenda for me but I felt like I had nothing to lose by going to the party. I still didn't really know where my head was following my break-up with London Girl.

As soon as I arrived at the dinner party I could tell exactly who James was trying to set me up with. If I had known at that point I had a type when it came to guys, he was it. Otto is incredibly handsome, tall with a shaved head, and Cambridge educated. He's calm and funny and I felt very relaxed around him. He also drove a Range Rover, owned two houses and had his own business, and to me, that shows independence and a strong business ethic, which are two things I find very attractive in a person.

We all got slightly drunk and Otto ended up kissing me that night. The stubble still felt weird – I had never snogged a girl with a beard.

Otto and I went on to spend a bit of time together. It was all very innocent – we were just hanging out as friends and going for dinner.

I didn't know what being gay was all about and I'm still slightly confused about it to this day. I've never even had sex with a guy.

I was quite confused about my emotions and wasn't sure how I was supposed to act – I knew how to be a boyfriend to a girl, but I didn't know if I needed to act differently with a guy. I know I come across as quite camp on the show, but back then I didn't think I was camp enough to be gay so I went out and bought a fake fur jacket, which I thought was the perfect accessory to make me gayer. I didn't realise that you could be gay but still act straight (no one ever tells you this stuff) and I didn't discover until quite late in the relationship that the reason Otto had liked me was because I wasn't as camp as some other gay guys. So I slightly fucked that one up, then. I wish someone had written a manual or a *Gay For Dummies* book. It would have made my life a lot easier.

Otto had an amazing flat in East London, and I remember leaving his house on a Sunday morning and walking down Shoreditch High Street when suddenly the heavens opened and it poured with rain. I have never seen rain like it – it was like something out of an apocalyptic movie. The church bells started ringing and for some reason I felt the happiest I'd been in a long time. I no longer felt alone. Being with Otto made me feel amazing: it was different, more like a friendship – a flatmate with something else thrown in for good measure.

* * *

Alex was the first person I told that I was sort of seeing a guy. He was amazing about it, and because he reacted so supportively, I slowly started to tell other people. I was pretty camp and flamboyant anyway so I don't think anyone was hugely shocked. I didn't tell my family at this point because I wanted to be totally sure about things before I said anything.

My biggest mistake was introducing Otto to someone as my boyfriend when I was drunk. That might sound odd, but in doing so people immediately started labelling me as a newly gay man. I found this very confusing because I hadn't quite figured out in my own head whether I was gay, bi or even an experimenting straight man. I didn't feel like I needed to put a label on myself, but the fact that other people were so quick to judge and put me in the 'gay' box put a lot of pressure on me and actually started to upset me a bit. Eventually that took its toll on my relationship with Otto and we drifted apart. We'd been seeing each other for three months, and with hindsight I can see it was such an important period in my life. Through Otto I was able to embrace this other side of my confused sexuality.

Until that point I'd been so consumed by women that I hadn't opened my eyes to what same-sex relationships would be like. Having a relationship with a man was a huge deal for me, but it felt right at the time and I wouldn't change what happened. It also showed me how your true friends will always love and respect you for who you are. You just have to trust them, and they also have to understand how difficult it may be for you. Alex and my flatmates were amazing.

A few years later I decided to give a relationship with a man one last chance to see how I really felt. That was with Ross, who I met on the club scene. He was South African and a model – tall, blond and amazingly well built. He was kind and funny, and so nice to me. He was everything I looked for – but he was everything I wanted in a *woman*.

Ross used to send me presents or a take-away so that when I got home there was a pizza waiting for me. He gave me a first-edition *Peter Pan* book because it's one of my favourites. But I found his beard terribly distracting when he kissed me. Of course the other guys I'd kissed had had a bit of stubble, but his was sharp and almost painful. It's quite off-putting when you're not used to it.

I tried to like him more, I really did. He was perfect – he just didn't have a vagina. We did all the usual things like going out for dinners and taking Sunday walks, but it just wasn't happening for me. After a few months we split up very amicably and I decided to have some time to myself to work out what I really wanted, instead of grabbing onto any kind of affection I could.

*   *   *

There is one famous gay guy I know that I'm incredibly drawn to, but would we work as a couple? Who knows. I certainly don't go for camp guys. All of the guys I like tend to come across as straight and he has something so special, maybe it'll happen some time in the future.

Some people have a problem because they can't pigeonhole me. I would say I was straight, but like 80 per cent of guys out there (including many that you would never imagine to have done so), have experimented with guys at one time or other. You'd be shocked at how many 'straight guys' come on to me! My advice is that if you do have a friend who is in a confused situation, just let them be whoever they want to be and be supportive, because I promise you that for them inside it's harder than it looks from the outside. They may smile through it – perhaps they'll become more extrovert – but in my experience that's just to cover up their insecurity. All they want is to be loved and supported.

CHAPTER 15

MAMMA MIA!

———

I'd come to be quite well known on the club scene as a result of working at 151, so I was asked if I wanted to host a night at Mahiki, a nightclub that's part-owned by Prince Harry's friend, Guy Pelly. Hosting involves running the door as well as making sure everyone is happy and the guests are well looked after. I loved it – I would spend the night chatting to lots of different people and getting paid for it, which for me is the perfect way to spend an evening.

One of the best things about working at Mahiki was the Treasure Chest cocktails they do. They are literally a vessel the size of a treasure chest filled with booze, mixers and fruit. Club promoting doesn't pay that well and London life is really expensive, which meant I was permanently broke, so I always made sure that I got my five-a-day by eating the fruit on the side of the treasure chest before I allowed myself to have any alcohol. I don't think it was the best way to try and stay healthy but at the time it worked nicely!

I put on nights for people like Lindsay Lohan and Emma Watson, and helped to host the *Mamma Mia!* premiere party. I had no idea what *Mamma Mia!* was because I hadn't seen the play or film, but it seemed to be a really big deal judging by all the fuss surrounding it and the press waiting outside.

There was an incredibly hot girl at the *Mamma Mia!* party who I couldn't stop staring at. She was so amazing that I decided I would be crazy if I didn't go up and ask for her number after all my relationship nightmares. My friends encouraged me to pursue her and as she was standing on her own it seemed like the perfect opportunity.

I put on my best strut in an attempt to look smooth (which I rarely pulled off) when suddenly this guy appeared and put his arm around her. I swiftly turned on my heel and walked back to my friends, tail between my legs. I was relieved that he arrived when he did or I would have been knocked back in front of the entire club. And I was even more relieved when I realised that they were in fact the two main stars of the show, Amanda Seyfried and Dominic Cooper. Amanda Seyfried was not that famous back then and so I had no idea who she was. At that point, they weren't officially out as a couple, but it was fairly obvious that she was taken. Can you imagine if I'd steamed in and tried to chat her up? Dominic Cooper, star of the movie of the moment and ridiculously good-looking man, versus a penniless club host whose last relationship was with a man. The humiliation would have been too much to bear.

Otto and I had been apart for a couple of months and I hadn't snogged, or even met, anyone that I liked for some time. With the exception of Amanda Seyfried, of course. Then one night in Mahiki I felt someone come up behind me and pinch my arse.

I turned around with the expectation of a balding older woman looking for a young man to show her a good time, instead to be faced with a girl who looked like a voluptuous Sienna Miller, with the same outrageously good body. I nearly had a seizure. She wore a white maxi dress with a flower headband – she was like a London nightclub-sent angel, with the most amazing boobs. For that reason, we shall call her Boho Girl.

I was desperate to impress her, but having no money all I could do was try to swindle her some free drinks – a tactic used by all club promoters, I must add. After arriving at her table with a tray of cocktails I had got for free in exchange for setting the barman up with Antalya, I went straight in and invited her round to mine for dinner the following evening.

I barely had enough money to eat let alone get any decent food, and the wine was the cheapest shit that cost £5 for *two* bottles and was probably not even made from real grapes – but the evening went surprisingly well and she even stayed the night. God knows why considering a) the state of the wine and the slightly burnt frozen salmon; b) the flat looked like we were squatters; c) my bedroom, which was so tiny that all that fitted into it was a single bed and a tiny cabinet, and it also stank of man and glowed like a Dutch brothel after Alex fitted red lights under the bed. It was the least sexy room you've ever seen in your life, which made the sex victory all the more amazing.

I was pretty convinced that mine and Boho Girl's night of passion would end up being a one-night stand. I would have been disappointed, but I couldn't really understand why she would want to go on another date with me having seen my hovel of a home and my bargain wine offerings. But, incredibly, she did, and we ended up dating for the next few months. She was the first Jewish girl I went out with and I've loved them ever since.

She had an air of naughtiness around her, which simultaneously excited and frightened me. I sensed that she might be a bit of a heartbreaker, so I held myself back a little from her. She was studying at Durham University, and while I visited her a few times, there was always the worry at the back of my mind that she might be being unfaithful. How could someone that gorgeous go to university and *not* snog loads of people?

Meanwhile, Richard, Alex and I were asked to take part in a TV show called *Natalie Cassidy's Real Britain*. Antalya was originally asked to do it because she was often featured as an 'It Girl' in Richard Kay's page in the *Daily Mail*, but a show like that is her idea of hell so she suggested us.

It was a series of six episodes about young Britons, and our episode was called 'Tradition about Aristocracy'. Of course, I was the token ridiculous non-aristocratic one on it, much as I am in *Made in Chelsea*.

We went to visit Brocket Hall as Alex's dad, Lord Brocket, was featured, and we also had to do an army assault course so we could experience what our forefathers would have done during their time in the Army. I was worried that I would come across as a total dick and I didn't want to be portrayed as the kind of guy I went to Cirencester with. But actually, it was fine, and we loved it. I asked the producers if they could keep me in mind for any other TV stuff as I had decided that I wanted to work in television.

A few weeks later the show came out and we'd planned to go to 151 to celebrate but Alex was too tired to come. In order to try to change his mind, I texted him saying, 'Alex, there are literally 30 women here who saw the show and they're loving it. You're missing out. I'm going to pretend I don't have a girl-friend tonight.' It wasn't true, I was just winding him up so he would come and join us and I thought the idea of 30 beautiful women would do the trick. Of course I thought it was hilarious, but sadly the joke was on me when I realised seconds after sending it that I had, in fact, sent it to Boho Girl. I spent the next half an hour drunkenly grovelling to her and trying to explain myself, but needless to say, it went down as well as you would imagine.

Over time, as much as I tried to tell myself I was over London Girl, I clearly wasn't. I thought about her a lot which, coupled with me not fully trusting Boho Girl, and now her not trusting me, meant that the relationship was doomed to fail before it had ever really begun. After one final trip to Durham, where I seem to recall suggesting we did role play in bed to save the sex life at least, we called it quits.

It seemed that I was destined to fail when it came to matters of the heart, so there was only one thing for it – it was time for me to return to my first love. The one who has always treated me right. Who has been there for me in my darkest hours. Yes, that's right: fish. Rather bizarrely, through hanging out at 151 I'd come to know a cab driver aptly called 'Ian the Fish', who would take you home for about £3. At the end of the journey he would open his boot and offer you a goldfish. He used to breed them and there would be hundreds of them in there, swimming around in plastic bags like you get at the fair. I always thought it to be quite rude to refuse, so there I'd be at five in the morning, alone, drunkenly carrying another goldfish into my flat. It was small compensation for a girl but at least I didn't wake up alone. You could tell how good a night you'd had when you woke up in the morning by whether or not you had a fish. If you had one, you'd got really drunk so it must have been a good night. If you didn't, you'd been sober enough to refuse. I used to have them in vases and all sorts, and in the end I had to go and buy a tank to keep them all in.

As fun as it might sound, the club scene was, in truth, pretty awful a lot of the time. I would often be found clearing up sick and collecting glasses. Someone once did a poo in a urinal and I had to put a glove on and pick it up. It was pretty rank.

We didn't have a uniform as such, but I had my standard self-styled wardrobe, which consisted of long hair, white jeans, cowboy boots and a shirt. I'll always look back on those days with great affection and over two years of being a cleaner I learned so much. But my dream of working in television was always at the back of my mind. And I really didn't ever want to have to pick up someone else's shit again!

💜 DEAR OLLIE: CLUBBING 💜

Clubbing and London go hand in hand. People flock to the capital's bright lights, where they dance the night away at clubs like Mahiki and Raffles. People will always love clubs, as will I. I did a lot of my growing up in them and they're somewhere I feel very comfortable. Almost at home, I guess. Like any business, the club scene has its secrets. And having worked on the door of many clubs and bars, I know most of them:

- The most important thing to remember if you want to get into one of the cooler nightclubs in London is that you need to demonstrate complete confidence without coming across as arrogant. Arrogance will not get you through the door, but you do need to apply a little bit of pressure. If you rock up to a club and just stand there waiting to be let in when there's a massive queue, it won't happen. You need to approach whoever is on the door and actually speak to them. In some clubs a £20 note in the back pocket often helps, because otherwise they'll happily leave you standing there for an hour and then tell you they are at capacity.

- The excuses that door hosts use most often – and which generally aren't true – are the following:

MAMMA MIA!

The club is at capacity
There are too many men in there already
It's over 21s night
They've got a private party on
It's members only

Nine times out of 10 these things won't be true. Another much-used phrase is 'please try our sister bar down the road'. This other venue is rarely affiliated with the club in any shape or form, but it's just a way to get people to go to another club.

- If I was working the door and someone came up to me and said, 'Ollie, darling!' and kissed me on both cheeks, I felt like I had to let them in because I had a connection to them. Even if they'd never met me before in their lives and someone had told them my name seconds earlier, I would assume I'd have met them before and that they might be someone really important. It's a very simple trick, but it works.
- Clothes are also very important. You have to know what you're dressing for. You're not going to get into a club if you're wearing a velour tracksuit. I'm not saying you have to be the most beautiful person in the world and be head to toe in designer clothes, but you need to have a certain attitude and look. Wear what you feel great in because that will give you the confidence you need to blag your way in. And confidence doesn't necessarily mean baring all

– just because you've got killer legs you don't have to wear a cheek-skimming mini dress that makes you look like Jodie Marsh circa 1994.

- When it comes to getting served at a crowded bar, don't start waving your money around in the air in an attempt to look flash. The people working behind the bar won't appreciate it. You need to let them see you're paying with cash because it's quicker than using a credit card and they also think you're more likely to give them a tip. But using your £50 note as a barman-luring flag will not work.

- Another tip is to make eye contact with one of the bar staff and hold it for as long as you can. Always stare at the same person. If you try to get the attention of too many people at once you're far less likely to get served. Focus on whoever is serving nearest to you and don't let them out of your sight. They will feel uncomfortable and want to serve you as soon as possible to get rid of you. Seriously, try it next time you're in a crowed bar.

- If you want to get in somewhere for free or get a table, you need to know the promoter. Some club promoters like to act as if they're loaded and important, but they can be a shallow lot and their friendship can usually be bought with good conversation over a few drinks. And once you've got an 'in' with them, you're usually sorted for future events, especially if you bring lots of friends along as you make his/her job easier, especially if they're a hot crowd.

People always used to call me and ask is there any way of getting another friend into the club? At the end of the day, that just puts another £5 in his pocket, so if you bring 100 people he/she'll be over the moon. Some clubs in London even offer a free dinner for 20, free drinks and entry, particularly if the clients are attractive and cool, because it makes the club look good.

- There's even a hierarchy with celebrities when it comes to clubs. Fame doesn't always offer you instant access, because you need the right kind of fame. Having said that, don't assume that all places around Chelsea are snobby or out of reach. Clubbing has changed a lot, especially around Chelsea. These days it's all about having fun. Some of the hottest places to go are the most down-to-earth. Bunga Bunga is a karaoke and pizza bar, and it's packed every night and booked up for months. Maggie's is Margaret Thatcher themes and 80s themed, Bodo's Schloss is based on a ski resort complete with a ski pod DJ booth and Mahiki is like walking into Hawaii (Mahiki actually means the Polynesian underworld). It's not all about aristocrats drinking bottles of vodka (although there is still quite a lot of that!). Above all, it's about having a good time and forgetting your troubles for the night.

CHAPTER 16

A LOVE POTION TO NEW YORK

I felt it was time to stop kissing frogs and find my future wife. Like in all good fairytales, I knew what had to be done: I needed a love potion. Thankfully the cosmetic shop Lush provided the answer to my prayers, with a heart-shaped bath bomb that has rose petals inside.

According to the instructions, when the sixth rose petal is released you make a wish, which will lead you to a lifetime of happiness. I can't believe I'm actually admitting this, but I bought so many of those bloody bombs that I lost count! Tina in the King's Road branch was very accommodating and I had so many baths in the vain hope they might actually work. Those were the actions of a desperate man. At least I didn't smell like a nightclub and was always incredibly clean. Now, I'm not sure it was anything to do with the love potion, but I did meet a girl soon afterwards who, to this day, I still regret losing.

I'd been invited to attend Polo in the Park with a group of friends. It's a three-day polo tournament that's held in Hurlingham Park at the Hurlingham Club in Fulham and it's enormous fun.

The royals were there and it was all fabulously posh. I love the royals and I've been lucky enough to meet a number of them over the years. In fact, I once taught Princess Eugenie how to use eyelash curlers. I was working on the door of a nightclub and she came over and asked me if my eyelashes were real. When I said they were, she asked how I got them to look like they did. Eyelash curlers, my darling. 'All you do is squeeze them together over your eyelashes for eight to ten seconds,' I said. 'You can get them in Boots!' My life was ridiculous.

Across the crowded bar at Hurlingham Park, I spotted a beautiful girl with long brown hair. All I could think was 'who the fuck is that? I have to meet her.' I swear she looked identical to Nina, my elusive older barmaid from Hayling Island. She was absolutely incredible. It wouldn't be long before I'd have to leave for work at 151, where I'd inevitably be clearing up sick, so I needed to go and ask for her number. But of course I didn't. I was far too scared of being rejected, Hattie Clarke style.

I may or may not have followed her for about 10 minutes or so but all I managed was a pre-pubescent, slightly squeaky 'hi!' when she walked past me. I didn't manage to build up the courage to say anything more and felt really bummed out about the fact that I would probably never see her again. I cursed myself the whole way to 151.

At the end of a hectic shift at the club, I stayed for a few drinks with the rest of the staff. At 4am we suddenly heard this loud thudding on the front door. I ran upstairs and could see that it was torrential rain outside. Through the window I could make out a female figure standing there dripping wet, trying to cover her hair with a pink pashmina. As I opened the door, she removed the pashmina in the same way that *Aladdin's* Princess Jasmine did in that market to the guards, and revealed herself to be the beautiful polo girl. If possible, she looked even more beautiful in her dishevelled state. Her rain-soaked dress clung close to her body, highlighting an amazing figure. It was like a scene from a fabulous rom-com – like *Four Weddings and a Funeral* without Andie MacDowell's slightly annoying voice. She said she was staying with her friend in the flat above the club but had been locked out, and asked if she could come in to shelter from the rain. Of course, I willingly obliged as I knew that I'd been given a second chance and I wasn't going to be stupid enough to miss this one. We got talking, she told me her name (but we shall call her Polo Girl) and that she worked in marketing – and that was the start of the most normal relationship I have ever had. We started texting and things progressed really quickly, despite it being difficult to see enough of one another because I worked nights and Polo Girl worked days. There was absolutely no drama. No worry. She liked me. I liked her. I met her family. She met mine. It was the type of relationship everyone dreams of. It was normal, and it could have been that way forever.

Then four months later, Polo Girl told me she wanted to go and live in New York for six months to work in fashion PR.

Of course, I was gutted – we hadn't known each other for long but I was happy – but I didn't want to stand in her way. We decided to try to make things work, with the help of Skype sex, but as with my previous long-distance relationships the miles did eventually split us up. Much in the same way as when I moved to London and grew apart from London Girl, Polo Girl felt like she had a whole new life to enjoy. We remained friends, but I always feel like she's one of the ones that got away.

I once said to her that the next guy she went out with after me she would marry, and she's now been in a very happy relationship for three years. It's probably only a matter of time, and I really hope he does propose because she deserves someone who will make her happy.

I've been in three relationships that I honestly thought could have ended in marriage. I know where

I want to be when I propose to the right girl: Port Quin, my favourite place in Cornwall. There's a little tiny lookout point there called Doyden Castle, which has the most incredible sea views and it's my hide-away from the rest of the world.

I love weddings, and in fact if I were to have a complete change of career then why not as a wedding planner? It's something I could definitely do as I know how to put on large-scale events having worked in clubs for so many years.

With Polo Girl off to the States, I hadn't got the fairy-tale ending my love bomb had promised me and I felt that life was slightly passing me by. I had a roof over my head, good friends and the work was regular, but being a club promoter doesn't have the most amazing prospects and my love life was dead in the water. Then two girls entered my life who were set to change it forever. Those girls were my Binky and Cheska. If you watch *Made in Chelsea* you will know that the three of us are inseparable. So it may surprise you to know that we only met for the first time four years ago.

I was organising a party in a bar on the King's Road and Cheska was the publicist. We got on from the word go, and I loved how opinionated and fiery she was, but also that she had a sweet side. She didn't take any crap and yet people still loved her.

She is one of the most amazing girls you'll ever meet.

She looked very different back then because she was a brunette. It was only when she later joined *MIC* that she went blonde.

We now live together and are so close but we do bicker in the same way that a brother and sister would. I can honestly say I have never met anyone who has as many unused beauty products or unworn clothes as Cheska. She's a real hoarder and refuses to throw anything away just in case she'll need it. I used to be like that (though I still have my sex capsule. You never know when the internet connection may go down).

Cheska lived with Binky, who back then was working for a property company. Slightly worrying, I know, but luckily it was not in infrastructure. I met her through a mutual friend and, hilariously, she was trying to be set up with me. Because she's so beautiful I was, of course, happy to oblige and I used my best flirting techniques on her, which generally involved sticking my finger up her nose – something that has never stopped.

We are a strong trio and even though we argue now and again, I couldn't live without them. I call them 'Tranny 1' and 'Tranny 2', and they're even programmed into my phone as that. It's not meant in a derogatory way, I just gave them the nicknames because they take so fucking long to get ready for a night out and each eyelash has to be perfectly in place in a way that only trannies or celebrities can get away with.

Without them I would probably have gone slightly crazy (OK, even more so). We've all got each other through difficult points in our lives and I know they're there anytime, day or night, if I have a problem.

They sometimes fight over me because they get jealous if one is getting more attention, which I secretly love. I have very different relationships with them both. Binky and I are always wrestling and my hands and her boobs are best friends, whereas Cheska and I are more civilised and our relationship is based on drinking wine and chatting. I guess it's a slightly more mature friendship. They're like my little sister and my big sister.

The three of us were all as skint as each other back then, so when one Sunday Binky and Cheska invited me over to their shared flat I took over Domino's pizza and some wine and we all got really pissed. Cheska went to bed to give Binky and I some alone time because it was so obvious that I liked her. Nothing had yet happened between us so while watching a shit film I strategically started to do the whole 'stretch your arm down the back of the sofa so you can move in closer' manoeuvre. I spent ages building myself up to go in for the kiss, but by the time I had plucked up the courage, closed my eyes and leant in, she was asleep.

I told her about it years later, and she said she would have kissed me back. Imagine how different things could be now? One night might have changed everything. One thing's for certain, our storyline in *Made in Chelsea* would be totally different.

CHAPTER 17

THE EMAIL THAT CHANGED EVERYTHING

———

I decided that Binky and I were better off remaining best friends and forgot about trying to woo her when another person you'll know very well from the show entered my life. I was working the door at Maggie's, which is a very famous 80s club on the Fulham Road, when a gorgeous girl walked past with long dark hair and extraordinary eyeliner. I was immediately fascinated by her.

Later on that evening we were introduced and we even flirted a little. I thought she had something very special about her, something you can't put your finger on.

I headed downstairs and about an hour later I heard a girl singing Phil Collins' 'Sussudio'. She had the most incredible voice; I had to know who it was. I looked across the crowded room to the small stage where, with a microphone in her hand, there stood the girl I'd been flirting with earlier in the night. I was totally mesmerised, as was everyone else in the room. And that, ladies and gentlemen, is how Gabriella entered my life.

She is a very well-respected pop star in her native Greece and has sold thousands of records. She was the manager's best friend and was booked to sing that night. She held that entire room in the palm of her hand – I've always found power so sexy.

Gabriella stayed behind after closing with the staff for a few drinks. I'd had a long night so I got stuck into a few manly vodka pineapples. While we were casually chatting, and emboldened by the booze, I thought 'fuck it' and did a drunken lunge. We ended up snogging in the corner of the bar and several hours later left the club together, completely shit-faced. I thought that maybe I was in a position to have my first bonafide one-night stand. My previous one with Boho Girl turned into a full-blown relationship so it didn't really count, and all my flatmates seemed to have them every day. It was something that I needed to get out of my system. Gabriella seemed up for having a night of fun so we hailed a cab and went back to mine.

As soon as we got in we grabbed some wine and navigated our way to my bedroom. We were lying on the bed kissing when she turned to me and said, 'I'm really worried that this is going to end up just being a one-night stand.' Shit.

Things progressed nicely. Dry humping and over-the-clothes groping quickly turned to actual bodily contact. I slowly slid my hand into her knickers when I suddenly felt this enormous mound of hair. In my drunken state, I started to feel quite ill; especially when the hair seemed never-ending in length. It was just so long and thick! In my head I was thinking 'I can't do this, I can't do this, this is horrendous', but how the hell was I supposed to get out of the situation? It was like some 80s rocker had decided to hibernate and die in her vagina. I honestly thought I was going to throw up.

I looked down at the foot-long vaginal mohican when I saw one of her clip-on hair extensions lingering between my fingers. It had come loose and somehow got entangled with her underwear during our dry humping session. Merkin-crisis averted!

We managed to get past the trauma of the fake hair and went on to have great sex. By the time I woke she'd already left and while I was sad that she didn't want to stick around, I was happy that I'd had my first no-strings-attached one-night stand. I almost felt violated ... in a good way. I'd been used. I felt alone and dirty. It was wonderful. It felt like I'd passed another milestone on my sexual journey.

It was my dad's 60th birthday that day and despite being hungover, of course I had to go. I suddenly had a flashback to 4am at Maggie's, several shots into it and me inviting Gabriella to be my date to the party. I decided to call her to check she had survived the Walk of Shame and also to make sure that it was just a bad dream that I had invited a complete stranger to meet my entire family.

But I felt so rough I couldn't face going to the party on my own, and I knew that having her there would show my family that I could actually get a girl. I'd taken girlfriends to my dad's birthday parties before but they had been proper, long-term girlfriends that I really liked and wanted to show off to everyone. There was only one problem: I didn't even know Gabriella's surname.

I stumbled around getting myself ready and meanwhile managed to persuade Barnaby, Alex and Cheska to come with me to help ease the awkwardness.

I was twitchy the whole way to the party, which was being held in the garden of Dad's house in Hayling Island. Of course, it was obvious to everyone from the look of terror on my face that I'd slept with Gabriella the previous evening.

A very large glass of Sauvignon Blanc later, I was feeling far perkier and ended up having a great day with Gabriella, so I asked her out on a date. I wasn't sure that she was the girl for me because my stomach didn't flip over when I looked at her, but I liked her a lot. Maybe my feelings would grow over time?

The bottom line is, you do kind of know if you 'like' someone or not, but feelings can grow. I found myself charmed and intrigued by Gabriella and that was the perfect base for a relationship.

Obviously if you go on five dates and you still don't like someone, there's just no point. Life's too short, so move on.

Gabriella and I went out for dinner a couple of times, and got along really well. She'd met my dad and his side of the family, so it seemed only fair that she met my mum too. Because neither of us had 9-to-5 jobs we had a lot of time to see each other, and we quickly became inseparable. We explored London, had weekends in Cornwall and spent months together with a spontaneous and carefree outlook. She is so much fun, and the sex was the best I've ever had. On one particularly memorable night out Gabriella and I were feeling particularly naughty while in a club on the King's Road. I was buying a round at the bar when she put her hand down my pants and started going for it. I was drunk and very keen and decided to go with the flow, and within about 10 minutes, we had jammed the bathroom door shut and were having sex. Now I finally felt I had accomplished the basis of an adult relationship.

We promptly left the club, hailed a taxi – in which we continued to be very naughty indeed – and fell through the door of my flat in Fulham, where we continued to go at it like rabbits in the corridor. After a while I could sense that someone was in the flat watching us really intently. I turned around to see

Alex sitting on the stairs, blind-drunk and smiling. He admitted to me the following day that he'd been so plastered that because of my long hair, as we fell through the front door he thought that we were a pair of magical lesbians sent by the drunken gods. It would have made his night! So he continued to watch.

That is really where it all started. We laughed a lot together and she got on well with all of my friends so she became a part of our group. We'd been together for six months when I received a phone call that would change everything.

It was October 2010 and my friend Antalya had been asked if she would be interested in taking part in a new reality show which would be screened on E4 and was focused around the real lives of people who live in Chelsea. Antalya couldn't think of anything worse, but Alex and I decided to go for it. It would prove a welcome distraction from clubs.

The show's producers came round to our house to film us, a couple more meetings followed, and in November I was told to wait for the email with their decision. By this point, Alex had decided against being in the show – his need and desire to be an entrepreneur was far greater than that for reality TV – but I didn't know what I would do if they said no. It was clear to me that I couldn't work in nightclubs forever, and the interview process had reignited my passion to be an actor. I waited anxiously for the news but I didn't want to feel the same kind of disappointment I did when I didn't get the role in *The Inbetweeners*. I was desperate for it to be a good outcome.

My father had just sold his property company, so to take my mind off everything he offered to fly me and two of my friends out to Thailand for a month's vacation to the island where he lived. I took along Gabriella and Barnaby, and every day I would leave them on Koh Phi Phi beach to go and use an internet café to check to see whether the email had arrived. On New Year's Day 2011, it was there. I had landed a part as one of the eight main characters on *Made in Chelsea*.

I sat there open-mouthed, staring at the writing on the screen that could change my life forever. It was the most incredible feeling. Even though my head was telling me not to get too carried away, that it might be a small show and I could be back working in the clubs in no time, in my heart I felt it was going to be the start of something special. But even then I could never have guessed that two years later the show would be aired in numerous countries around the world, and that it would be the biggest adventure I'd ever embarked upon.

The email stated that it was strictly confidential and that I couldn't tell anyone. Because of this and the fact that I didn't know what was going to happen to us, I didn't tell Gabriella for three days. It was hard to keep it to myself, but when I did tell her the news she was so proud of me and I felt really emotional. I told my dad over breakfast the following day and he was over the moon. I had to swear them both to secrecy. It felt like it was the beginning of something new and incredible.

I think they planned on getting a lot of press attention as it would compete with the already huge reality show, *The Only Way is Essex*. Despite being ecstatic at the news, while on holiday I realised that things between Gabriella and me were not great. We had spent too much time together. It had all become too much too soon. I knew that I had found someone who would give me everything I had ever wanted. She was kind, sweet and funny, but something just wasn't working for me. She was almost too adoring, to the point where it began to get a bit suffocating. It sounds terrible, I know, particularly as I'd also been on the receiving end of being told I was too nice, but it was almost too easy and I got bored. It's not that I'm not a big one for game playing, and I don't think for a minute that you should mess people around, but if you're in a relationship you do want to be kept on your toes. I know a couple who have been married for 45 years and every now and again the wife won't pick up her phone when her husband rings, just to keep him interested. Gabriella was the total opposite.

I wanted to have to do some of the chasing but Gabriella gave everything.

I pushed my concerns to the back of my mind and distracted myself with the adventure that was about to start. When the *Made in Chelsea* bosses found out I had a girlfriend they were keen for her to appear on the show as they wanted to cover all aspects of our lives. Gabriella promptly agreed.

Rather than fill me with excitement that we'd be on this journey together, I felt slightly worried. I spoke to my mum that night and explained how I felt about her, to which she very firmly, and very wisely, said, 'Do not hurt this girl. Do not break up with her on the show. Do it before the show starts.'

But I convinced myself that things would be OK and that this new chapter in our lives would bring us closer together. How wrong I was …

CHAPTER 18

LAID IN CHELSEA

———

We started work on *Made in Chelsea* in early February 2011 and it was absolutely mind-blowing. None of us – Binky, Gabs and Cheska – had any idea what it was going to be like. Binky and Cheska were offered to appear in the show at the same time as me, which was amazing as in the past year they had become my two closest girl friends.

We thought the show might end up being similar to *Shipwrecked*, another E4 show, and that it would just be a one-season thing that people would watch and then forget about. We could never have predicted how popular it would become.

I soon met the other cast members, like Mark Francis, who I thought was the most ridiculous man I had ever met – in the best possible way. We got talking and soon realised that we had a friend in common: Pedro, my next-door neighbour in Cambridge, who famously had my name tattooed into his arm. I also met Fredrick for the first time and he is without a doubt one of the nicest people you can ever meet in your entire life.

I already knew quite a lot of the other cast, like Amber, Spencer, Hugo, Caggie and Millie, thanks to the Chelsea club scene. In fact, I first met Millie when she was 18 years old and was working for Richard's magazine. I had hired her to be a make-up artist for one of the front covers and I've still got her original business card with 'Camilla Mackintosh, make-up artist' written on it.

I think we were all very wary of each other at first. We were all going to feature on the show but we didn't know what one another was about – or who was being a dick about other people behind closed doors. It would be months before we saw the first episode, so we had no idea about who had big parts or if people were out to get us. It was quite unnerving, but in the end I was just myself. I didn't want to play games, I just wanted to have fun, be with the girls and make people laugh.

When I look back now we've all changed so much since the beginning of the show. It's only been just over two years and four seasons but we look completely different for starters. Spencer used to have a slicked-back mullet and I, of course, still had my long hair.

One thing we did all have in common was that we were terrified we were going to be set up to look like complete dicks, like a bunch of spoilt and shallow rich kids. Not that some people don't do that well enough on their own (not mentioning any names), but we didn't want to look like horrible arseholes because that's just what most of the cast aren't. I had given up my job for the show, and it would have been very hard to get another one if I looked like a complete dick.

Despite my concerns, I was incredibly excited about the first day of filming. I turned up to Raffles and was greeted by the filming crew. We were all a bit wide-eyed and I was totally clueless about what would unfold. Caggie, Millie, Hugo and Spencer all arrived together, and I remember thinking that they must have small parts as they weren't at any of my meetings with the producers and the confirmed cast. As it turns out, what would we have done without them? In the end the first day of filming went great and Binky, Cheska and I obviously used the occasion as an excuse to go out for a drink afterwards. We dissected everything and celebrated what we hoped would be the start of something new. We had no idea then that it was to become so popular.

At first it took a little while for people to warm to the show. This meant that fame wasn't instant for any of us, which was good because it wasn't a massive shock to the system when we did start to get recognised. It didn't take long for viewers to become hooked, though, once the word got out.

Watching the show back on TV was – and still is – the hardest thing in the world. We have a regular thing where we all get together on a Monday night in a club on the King's Road and watch the programme together, while drinking lots of wine, of course.

It was weird seeing ourselves on TV that first time and we all sat there cringing at everything we said and did. Had it not been for several glasses of wine I'm not sure some of us would have been able to get through it all.

I was very nervous about how the public and press would react once *MIC* was unleashed, as there has never been anything positive shown about posh people, except perhaps Hugh Grant. But, on the whole, the reception was great.

There was one instance, however, that showed the nastier side of being on TV. I was on my way to Cheska's birthday party at the Sanctum Soho Hotel, and I was walking there with Aliona Vilani from *Strictly Come Dancing* who was living next door to me at the time. I lent her my Union Jack jacket because she was cold and then a group of paps started taking photos of us. Out of nowhere a guy grabbed my face and tried to punch me. Not one of the paps tried to help me, they just carried on snapping. It made me realise how ridiculous this life can be. Some random guy was assaulting me and all the photographers cared about was getting the photo. I managed to push the guy off and get into a taxi, and ridiculously all I could think about once I was safe was what excellent shoes the attacker had on. If you're going to be manhandled, you at least want the man to be smartly dressed.

Gabriella joined the show right from the beginning and we were the first relationship on *Made in Chelsea*, but about a month into filming my doubts about us began to resurface.

She took me away skiing for my birthday, but at that point I could not envisage Gabriella and me on a romantic holiday in the Alps. So I invited Binky and Cheska along to make it more of a casual group thing. Needless to say, it did not go down well when they turned up out of the blue, intruding on Gaby's romantic gesture.

We did have a lot of fun, though, skiing all day and eating fondue. But you always know when a relationship is going downhill when the slightest little thing annoys you. Gaby had this habit of turning around to me and saying 'Faaaaaaaace' whenever she wanted a kiss. I remember skiing along one day and she started doing it and I just thought 'how annoying'. It went from being vaguely cute to incredibly irritating within a matter of weeks.

There was no way I could keep up the façade for another 10 weeks of filming. It was all going so wrong between us and I knew I needed out. Soon.

A few weeks later I was having dinner with one of my favourite *MIC* producers near my home. We were just having a laugh over a few bottles of wine when Gabriella called. She wanted to know when I would be finished so she could meet me, and then she insisted on picking me up from the restaurant.

When she turned up she had *the* most furious look on her face for absolutely no reason. She'd mistakenly believed I was having dinner with my sister and so was upset, suspicious and insecure despite the producer and me being just friends.

Gaby and I went back to her place, where I said as gently as I could, 'I don't want to be in this relationship with you anymore.' We both sat there crying and weirdly decided to listen to the band Lady Antebellum on repeat.

When I woke up the following morning she was still obviously very upset and I felt like the biggest arsehole in the universe. I was gutted too, but in my heart I knew it was the right thing to do. As I went to leave she walked over to her dressing table, picked up a make-up brush and handed it to me, saying, 'Here, take it. You've been looking for one this good for ages. Have it to remember me by.' To be fair, it was an amazing brush and I did need one so, awfully, I took it. In fact it was one of the best break-up mementoes I've ever had. Including U2's best album.

We'd had a few days to think about things and cool off when Alex persuaded me to take her for dinner and make one last go of things. He thought we were a good match and he didn't want me rushing into ending things on a whim.

We did rekindle our romance briefly, but that was a mistake, and we ended up splitting up again on camera only a week later, which was far worse than the original break-up. We were at a charity evening on a boat and we went on deck to talk. In truth, I think we both knew how the night was going to end. I couldn't look at her because I knew how much I was going to upset her and I felt *awful*. We were both so nervous because breaking up is hard enough, let alone on camera with a whole crew watching such an intimate moment. It was the first break-up on *Made in Chelsea*, but obviously not the last.

But at the end of the day, I knew it had to be done, and when I woke up the next morning I felt horrendous but also an overwhelming sense of relief. Of course I still cared immensely about Gabriella and wanted her to be OK, which, rightly or wrongly, I'm going to use as an excuse for why I ended up sleeping with her several times following our split. In retrospect, it was wrong and it goes against everything I believe in. I have no explanation for why we did it, but the needy part of me wanted some company and, shamefully, sex. And we did have great sex.

But our drunken fumbles were to become a thing of the past, and I was ready to move on. Little did *MIC* audiences know then that my next love interest would be a guy.

CHAPTER 19

THE SECRET

———

Shortly after Gaby and I split up I sat down with some of the producers to talk about this recent change in my life. I told them that I had dated a couple of guys in the past, and that this may well have had something to do with my break-up with Gaby. I thought long and hard about whether I wanted to share this side of my life with the producers, my family, friends and old teachers, who still didn't know about my past relationships with guys.

Discussing this in the show meant that I wasn't going to have a straightforward coming-out story, I would be doing this in front of two million people, including everyone I have ever dated and been to school with.

I had seen friends coming out to their parents over the years, and I knew how hard they found it.

215

I decided that if I was going to do this – come out on national TV – I wanted it to have a big impact to help other gay or bisexual men and women who may be struggling to accept who they are. I've heard such awful things about people feeling completely tortured because they can't talk to anyone about their sexuality. What kind of an example would I have set if I'd lied about who I was?

I knew my mum had to be the first person I told, and I chose to tell her by the Peter Pan statue in Kensington Palace Gardens, because it's one of my favourite places in London.

I felt both terrified and happy that I was finally going to get this off my chest. I had no idea how she would react.

We had a lovely walk around the park before I guided her to the statue. I stood there for about three minutes not really knowing what to say. Eventually I turned to her and said, 'Mum, I love you. I feel there comes a point in my life that I need to be completely honest with you.'

After a long pause I said, 'I'm not sure how I feel about guys and girls, I think I might quite like them both.'

Mum was amazing about it and even said, 'Let's open the champagne!' I couldn't have loved her any more in that moment. She made me so proud. We were both very emotional and she hugged me and it really couldn't have gone better.

That same evening I sat my dad and sister down to tell them everything. It was the last thing they expected to hear, but like Mum they were totally fine about it.

I later filmed a scene at my flat with Binky where I talked about my bisexuality, and I even went on a date with a guy. I felt that it was important to address my sexuality on the show, and hope that by doing it I've helped others embrace who they really are.

Made in Chelsea has changed my life and enabled me to do things that I would never have had the chance to do. Like giving talks and debates at both Cambridge and Oxford Universities, which are two of my proudest moments of the last few years.

Having gone to drama school in Cambridge, the city will always have a special place in my heart, so I was thrilled to be invited back to take part in a debate at the Cambridge Union.

We were up against the Footlight students in a comedy debate entitled: 'I'd rather live in Cambridge than Chelsea'. I was asked to put together a small team of people from *MIC*, so I chose Mark Francis, Freddie and Francis Boulle. I wanted us to be a comedy team: Freddie is very, very clever, Francis is a dry intellectual and Mark is hilarious. It was the perfect combination.

I was shocked at how many people came along to watch the debate – it was apparently one of the biggest turnouts they'd ever had. Who knew – top-flight academics also like reality TV!

The whole thing was such fun; it was set in the Cambridge debating chambers, and each team had to get up and put forth its reasons for why it should win the debate.

When it was my turn to speak I made a joke which seemed to go down well. I talked about my time in Cambridge and how I'd taken part in the Varsity Ben & Jerry's eating competition, after which I ended up with my head so far down the toilet I could see Oxford. That ended up getting more of a laugh than anything else.

After the debate I was approached by a young English student that we will call Chrissie. She was blonde and had a face like a china doll, and I remember being struck by how incredibly beautiful she was.

When she said her name was Chrissie I thought she said Cressida, which is the name of one of the characters in a Shakespeare play I had recently read. OK, fine, listened to as part of a Radio 4 comedy play once. When I asked her why her parents would name her after a cheating slut, she smiled a knowing smile and said, 'My name is actually Chrissie and I won't study *Troilus and Cressida* until next year.' I was well and truly put back in my box.

At that point I decided it was time to whip out the monologue that Troilus vents to his friend after Cressida betrays him. I decided that it would prove that I wasn't just a reality TV idiot but an academic with a penchant for sixteenth-century playwrights, even if it was untrue.

It seemed to work as we arranged to meet at Cindy's, the legendary local club at which I'd snogged the Polish cleaner all those years ago. I ended up doing shots at the bar with one of Chrissie's friends, Toby. He ran the punting in Cambridge, so at midnight we snuck out, unlocked the boats and started punting down the River Cam fuelled by a bottle of tequila and candles. We had a blanket on our legs, which is perfect for a snuggle grope, and one thing led to another and Chrissie and I ended up kissing.

It was 6.30am and I was filming later on that day. I met Cheska in a bookshop and pretended that I had stayed in the night before, when in fact I smelt so bad that I was offered a Smint by the owner of the shop. She disguised it as a welcome gesture, though I'm fairly sure it was because I smelt like an alcoholic. Chrissie loved the show and gave me her granny cardigan to wear for my next scene, which happened to be the one in which I first mentioned my desire to write this very book.

Chrissie and I stayed in touch and ended up seeing each other for a while. I loved the fact that I had an excuse to go back and forth to Cambridge again and I made the journey every other weekend, even taking the train just so I could feel like a proper student again. If I have one regret in life it's that I didn't work my arse off at school and try to get into Oxbridge rather than go to Cirencester. I will always have a huge place in my heart for Cambridge but sadly it wasn't to be with Chrissie.

Eventually, as is often the way, the visits became more infrequent, along with the texts to one another, which before long stopped altogether. I admit that is an easy and lazy way to avoid a break-up, though I still think under certain circumstances it is an acceptable way to do things.

Female friends of mine say they would much rather a guy told them straight that he didn't want to see them again instead of just not texting or calling, but I think it softens the blow a bit. I guess you have to gauge it according to the person and the relationship, but personally I would rather things just fizzle out than make a dramatic statement. I would find it very hard to say to someone: 'I'm just not that into you'.

Not long after things ended with Chrissie, I met someone else – an amazing girl who I really fell for. She was kind and loving and anyone would be lucky to be in a relationship with her. An incredible summer passed and she came onto the show for the second season, so if you watched it you'll know who she is, but for various reasons I've decided not to go into detail about her or our relationship here.

However, as we got further into the series, it became very clear that Gabriella was still hung up on me. We were both trying to move on but when I started to spend more time with my new girlfriend, problems arose. I ignored Gabriella's phone calls and voicemail messages for the first time ever and it eventually came to the point where I knew I would have to explain myself to her. So one afternoon a few weeks later I sat Gaby down, face to face, and told her that I was seeing someone else, and that I really liked her. I later found out she called Cheska in tears. I hated the fact she was upset, but it wasn't like I was going out of my way to hurt her. I wanted the best for her and was desperate for her to meet someone amazing and be happy.

It was my fault entirely. I should never have carried on sleeping with her; it only gave her hope that we would continue as we were all those months ago in Thailand. We hadn't spent any time apart and we had carried on as though we were still together, but the sad thing was that, for me, it was over the day I met my new girlfriend.

When my new relationship became official, Gabriella found it very difficult. She was still in love, and whether through jealousy or wanting attention, she became harder to get along with. She was clearly really fucked up about the whole situation and it must have been awful to see her ex's public relationship playing out on the *Daily Mail* online. But the difficulty was that she had become good friends with my friendship group. She hadn't known them before we got together, and normally when a relationship ends you go back to the friends you had before. But Gaby had become best friends with Binky and Cheska, she wore a Union Jack dress to a premiere and became very friendly with my sister. She even went to stay at my dad's house for a weekend. Then there was that infamous music video with several lookalikes of me. I didn't know what to think. I just wanted to focus on my relationship and at that time nothing else mattered.

It was around about this time that Gaby's relationship with Cheska got really awkward. Even though they were good friends, Cheska's loyalty would always lie with me, and so she would fight my corner when Gabs was making things difficult about my new relationship.

One night it all got really tense. Cheska and Gabs were outside Maggie's and they were talking about the fact that I was seeing someone new. Gabriella got very emotional and started crying and asking how I could do it to her.

Cheska listened but she said that something inside her clicked that night and she knew she had to tell Gaby some home truths because enough was enough.

She basically told her the truth; that we were never getting back together, and she needed to realise that sooner rather than later. They ended up screaming at each other on the streets of Chelsea, and walking off in separate directions, which was the start of things going very sour between them.

Their friendship was up and down for a while after that and even up until recently they were having a few 'moments', shall we say. But everything changed in the last six months and now Gabs is over it all. She decided to leave Chelsea and the show, and now she has started a new life in LA.

Even without all that drama, the course of true love never runs smooth – particularly for me – and after seven months my new girlfriend and I broke up. I was devastated. But that is one relationship I'm keeping to myself.

♥ DEAR OLLIE: SEEING YOUR ♥ EX FOR THE FIRST TIME

Now there are few things more awful than seeing your ex for the first time after that hideous break-up, and you can rest assured that it will be either on your first Walk of Shame – unbrushed, unshowered, hungover and on a bacon and egg run to Tesco on Sunday morning – or if you are really unlucky it will be on your third date with the guy you ended up on a blind date with after the office party. Only once or twice in the history of relationship stories has there been the perfect ex run-in – the infamous one where you just happen to be helping an injured model across the road while on the way to a black tie ball, having just got out of the Ferrari you won for the day in the office tombola.

Let's face it, usually it happens when most of us look awful, and we are picking out gherkins in Asda with our completely un-sexual friend.

So here are some pointers to help you get through those purely hideous moments that you will inevitably encounter!

- The most likely scenario is that you will see him or her while shopping, hungover, at Tesco on Sunday. This means that the chance of them being with a new prospective partner is greatly increased. If this happens, avoid the aisles that show you to be a desperate spinster or merely a lonely man, as their new partner is undoubtedly perfect. Rule out the loo roll, vaginal hygiene products, chocolate, wine and dental floss and instead aim for the boxes of condoms, the salad, cucumber (makes them think of a penis, works for both sexes) and sparkling water – even if you don't like it, buy it, it makes you look sophisticated.

- Whatever happens, do not cry and hide behind a trolley eating a chocolate mousse – it's never a great look.
- Always make sure you look amazing before you leave the house, and if you look like shit, just blame it on the fact that you were up all night (they'll know what you mean).
- Remember if you are in a supermarket then you have an abundance of products around you that will make you look better, so dash to the make-up aisle and grab a bronzer, then let them know that you have been on holiday with the girls/guys.
- If you happen to run into your ex in a nightclub, this is dangerous, because you are under the influence of the one substance that will make you emotional, have low inhibitions and, to make matters so much worse, it even makes people better-looking. In this situation, avoid your ex at all costs. If you must, kiss them on both cheeks and then head for the dance-

floor as quickly as possible. Do not ponder or even let your mind think about how good the sex used to be.

- If you run into them when you're on a date, this is awkward, but for you it's also the dream. It shows you are moving on and other people want to have sex with you, which is wonderful and will drive your ex mad with jealousy.

- If you run into your ex while he/she is on a date, smile and walk away. Don't cry (yet), just go and get a bottle of your favourite alcohol, then head home and get drunk with friends. YOU ARE ALLOWED TO DO THIS!

CHAPTER 20

HAIR TODAY

It was really hard to go through another break-up on the show, and by the time Series 3 came around I found myself single and hating it. That series was a really strange one for me. After the emotional roller-coaster of break-ups in the first two series, I wanted to take a bit of a back seat and just do what I always wanted to do, which is make people laugh. All I wanted was to have memories of an amazing experience that I could keep forever, no matter where I might end up later on.

Before starting the show Binky was in a relationship with a Chelsea boy but they broke up before filming began. Binky was understandably devastated and in the hope of moving on she took the opportunity to go on a date with Spencer. Nothing happened between them, but that was the start of Binky and Spencer becoming very close friends.

I have to admit, Cheska and I found that quite hard. I don't see Spencer very often and we aren't close friends, although we'd occasionally see each other through the show and get along well. So when in one episode Binky turned to Spencer and said, 'You can be my new Ollie Locke', I was devastated. It ripped me apart, though Binky and I have never actually spoken about it. She is amazing because she's so laid-back, which is why it's never felt right to raise it with her. She wouldn't have meant it, it wouldn't have even crossed her mind she might have upset me. She's so chilled out that she'll turn up on the set of *MIC* in tracksuit bottoms. It was perfect when in one episode she turned up to a pyjama party in a scruffy old T-shirt when all the other girls were wearing ridiculously skimpy underwear they had bought from Agent Provocateur. I love that about her. She loves dressing up, but at the same time she's happiest in a holey jumper and some leggings. That's how I prefer her; she still looks amazing and I think everyone watching the show can see that's how she is. After doing *Made in Chelsea* for three years, I have *never* heard one bad word said about Binky. The whole country loves her, as they bloody well should! Binky and Cheska are my rocks; we're always there for one another and I can't think of many other people I'd want to spend so much time with. In fact I don't seem to be able to live without them – and I'm still living with them now, well, one of them …

During season one, I lived with the guys in the flat that boasted the famous roof terrace and the Gabriella 'if you were stuck on a desert island, I'd call 999' front door. But there came a point when I decided that it was time to grow up and buy my own place – which was terrifying as only a year before my mum had been bailing me out of parking tickets and Congestion Charge fines.

I looked around for months to find something I knew I could make my first home. Eventually I walked into a place in an amazing complex and knew I'd found exactly what I wanted.

In October 2011 I moved in. I really only wanted a few things to start off with – I always thought that if I had a Molton Brown hand soap and a Jo Malone candle I would feel like the house owner I wanted to be. But then I decided to scour London to find black and white wallpaper and I covered the whole flat in it. My sitting room looks like a hideout for a cartoon robber who's holding a large gold mirror he's stolen. You might have seen it on the show …

It was awesome having my own home and being able to do what I liked. No one bought blue loo roll because it was cheaper! But not long after Cheska and Binky, who were still living together in Parsons Green, were told that their rental agreement was coming to an end, so I offered both of them the spare room in the flat. They ended up flipping a coin for it, and as you probably know, Cheska won.

Around the same time my Granny Hatton became very ill, and within weeks she sadly passed away. My mum then decided that she wanted to move to London, so in the most extraordinary of circumstances, Binky and my mum ended up moving in together.

Series 3 passed by in a blur. Richard Dinan joined the cast and it was great to have another friend on the show. But, all in all, I wasn't in a good place at that time. My previous break-up was still taking its toll, losing my grandmother was very hard and I started to feel that I had become a bit of a parody of myself. By the time the summer of 2012 and filming for Series 4 came about, I realised that I hadn't had any form of relationship – let alone a good shag – in over nine months. This wasn't a fact I felt particularly happy about. I began to question what the problem was and realised that I no longer really knew who I was. Despite only snogging a few men over the years compared to 10 relationships with women, the whole country thought I was 100 per cent gay.

I needed to make some changes. Big changes. I'd had long hair since I was 16 and I needed a new look. My hair had grown longer and longer, and become my trademark. When you work in clubs you have to look different and be recognisable, and having long brown hair helped.

But after a while I felt that I had lost my sense of self. I was no longer Ollie Locke, I was 'Ollie from *Made in Chelsea*' – the guy with the long hair and Union Jack clothing. Something had to give. I looked at myself in the mirror and realised that I wasn't happy with what I saw any more. Plus, if I was going to end this horrific nine-month sex drought then it would probably make sense to do something about my hair.

After all, if you ever ask a girl what type of man she goes for, she rarely says 'Mediterranean camp guys with long hair'. Especially girls who live in Chelsea. Not that I'm saying my hair was the sole reason why I wasn't having sex, but I felt like it may have been one factor in the package that had knocked my confidence with the ladies.

I had one big problem, though – my ears. When I was a kid I hated my ears so much I thought that – along with wanting to look like a cross between Travis, Charlie and Jarred – by growing my hair I could deflect attention away from them.

There was only one thing to do; I called a Harley Street clinic and booked myself in to have my ears pinned back. I had to be awake throughout the operation, which was rather terrifying, although it didn't hurt during the procedure and 111 Harley Street is renowned for being the best at ears, so I was in safe hands. It was bloody painful for a couple of weeks afterwards as they were healing, but it was worth it to be able to look in the mirror and not hate what I saw.

So then I decided it was time to cut off the hair. This was difficult for me. Was I really going to lose those locks that I'd spent the past 10 years growing? I told the show that I wanted to cut it and they nearly had a seizure. I booked an appointment at Neville in Belgravia and the cameras followed as the first cut was made, and my long dark hair fell to the pristine white floor. I held my breath and stared straight into the mirror. I was so ready for it but also so scared. As soon as it was done, I felt a weird sense of relief and I was thrilled with the result. I donated my hair to a charity called the Little Princess Trust in Brighton that makes wigs for children who have lost their own hair due to cancer. It's already been made into a wig so somewhere a little girl is wearing my hair, and that means the world to me.

Just to top everything off, I threw out most of my clothes (apart from my Union Jack stuff, of course!).

I was still me, but I didn't feel like I was a complete joke any more.

A few days later the producers of the show called to speak to me because they were genuinely worried I was going through some kind of silent breakdown. I think Cheska may have been thinking the same thing too. But actually I was probably the sanest I'd been in my life; I was seeing things more clearly than I had done in a long while.

I was really happy with my new look, and by the time Series 4 started, about a month later, most people had begun to get used to it. On the whole I got a great reaction, but some people were surprisingly weird. I've had comments like 'You've ruined yourself now you've cut your hair.' Can you imagine ever saying that to anyone, especially to their face? When I reply, 'Actually I did it because I was really unhappy with myself,' they don't know what to say. Just because most of the time I come across on screen as happy and ridiculous doesn't mean I don't have my down days and insecurities like everyone else. I'm lucky that I don't suffer with that many bad comments on Twitter. I'm not a dick and I don't set out to offend people. That said, I did once get a message from someone saying they were going to hunt me down and stab me with an infected needle. I was devastated but decided that the best thing to do would be to just bat it off, but the knowledge that someone has sought you out and put finger to keyboard with the specific intention of abusing you is hard to accept sometimes.

* * *

By the time the new series got into full swing I felt completely reinvigorated. I started dating again and began to do all of the things that I had been missing so much.

My new look had given me a much-needed confidence boost and it is well known that if you feel good about yourself then you attract people to you like a magnet.

We all fear change, but making those changes in my life made such a huge difference to how I felt about myself. Of course change has to come from the inside too, if that doesn't sound too worthy, but you shouldn't let other people's opinions hold you back from changing things about yourself you're unhappy with. If you live your life for other people you will never truly be happy. Many people tried to talk me out of cutting my hair or told me my ears were fine, but it's all about how *you* feel. If you want to make a change, make it.

CHAPTER 21

HATTIE, *TOWIE* AND A TRIATHLON

I started writing this book in 2011, and it's been like love therapy for me. Revisiting past relationships in detail now I'm older and wiser has shown me what mistakes I've made and how I'd do things differently now. It's like looking at my history as an outsider, which has helped me to work out what I do and don't want in a relationship going forward. I'd been writing for almost a year and was updating my friend Toby on its progress. I lamented how I hadn't had a date in so long that I'd forgotten how to be in a relationship, which seemed ridiculous since I was writing a book about relationships. 'What you need is to go on another date. I know a girl who will be up for it,' he replied. Great, I thought, he's going to set me up with an ugly horny girl or one of his sloppy seconds or someone that breathes too deeply in her sleep.

Googling my date-to-be, I saw that she looked hot externally, no sign of hideous skin condition or a lazy eye, and that she used to be in a big TV soap about five years ago. I remembered her from those days but she looked far more beautiful now and she was at that time a major voiceover artist.

I had nothing to lose by going on this date, except my virginity, which had seemingly grown back after my undeserved chastity. It was Halloween and Toby set us up on a blind date in a club in Kensington. We got on surprisingly well from the word go; luckily she was dressed in something more slutty than a corpse bride and we ended up having a bit of a snog that night. We started seeing each other more regularly and we were messaging constantly. It was that kind of amazing constant BBM banter, where everything is hilarious and you end up smiling like an idiot while you sit on the loo, in the bath or on the Tube. We had the same sense of humour, which is one of my priorities when it comes to girls. I knew I hadn't had such a sense of humour connection on this level since Tilly, way back at school, which was a genuine worry to my heart. But, that said, the relationship did have its issues.

She was convinced that I was sleeping with loads of people like some of the other cast mates she knew did. The reality was that I hadn't had sex in so long that the 65-year-old woman who gives out free chocolate samples in my local M&S was starting to look dateable. I just acted aloof to keep her on her toes in the hope that she would fall for my fake Lothario 'I could get with whoever' attitude. It failed, and it was another lesson learned.

Despite these issues, Soap Girl, as we will call her, and I got on ridiculously well. We spent every day together exploring London, and we laughed constantly. After only three months I knew that I was dangerously close to falling for her. But one thought troubled me: if I brought her onto *MIC* and lived our relationship in the public eye as I had done twice before, it was bound to fuck up. I'd end up crying to a relationship guru in India for the next 20 years before realising I was gay after all!

I just couldn't face having another relationship on camera. After the last one ended, I had cried more than I had ever done and it had taken me months to feel even slightly better. And it wouldn't be fair to me or her to pretend that I wasn't seeing anyone and to carry on doing the show as normal without anyone knowing. I had to make a decision, and sadly it was to be single. So, with a heavy heart, the following Sunday morning, over brunch, I ended it. A decision that I would later realise was a huge mistake. All my friends loved her – we were perfect.

As harsh as it sounds, I went about removing her from my life – deleting her from my Facebook and Twitter accounts, all the normal things I do after a break-up. It was months later and the new series was nearly out, my love life was completely useless, sex was something I could just about remember and two sad singletons (Cheska and myself) sat down to watch the advert announcing the new series of *MIC* on E4 – to discover that the voiceover artist was none other than Soap Girl. I'd done everything I could to prevent myself from seeing or hearing about her and of course she had bloody well landed a job on my show! You may have noticed that things are never normal around me – and there was no escape. And, as it soon appeared, there was no escaping Hattie Clark either.

One Sunday afternoon Binky popped round for tea, OK, fuck it, wine. She was outside when her phone rang so I answered – to hear Hattie Clark's voice. It was the last person I was expecting. I hadn't seen or spoken to her since that embarrassing incident in Cornwall. I knew that Binky and Hattie's paths had crossed in the past, but I had no idea they were now friends. I don't know whether she remembered our cringeworthy run-ins, but she was being really over-friendly and invited Binky and me round to her house that night for drinks. I pretended to be completely cool about seeing her again and for once I felt like I was almost cool enough to be chilling with the infamous Hattie. It was a great evening, and we stayed up drinking, laughing and chatting until 4am. I got so drunk that I thought I would send out a tweet that read, 'If anyone out there wants to tell someone they love them, do it now. Or if you fancy someone, ask them out.' (If I wasn't getting laid then I could at least try to inspire someone to get the confidence to get some.) Hattie read it, turned to me and said, 'Ollie, will you go out with me?'

I laughed and said something inappropriate, thinking she was joking, but it became apparent that she wasn't. I reminded her of how uncool I was (why after 10 years of trying to get her I was trying to put her off, I have no idea). The next night, I got us a table at one of my favourite restaurants called La Bodega Negra, on Old Compton Street in Soho. I'm not going to lie, I was shitting myself knowing I may finally have a chance to snog the woman who had been my dream-girl and mean-girl all that time ago.

I described that painful scene and told her that she'd acted like a dick, to which she replied, 'Yep, that sounds like me.' I was sort of expecting a kiss and for her to say she would make up for it in other ways, but annoyingly she's very blunt and she just laughed it off.

The evening got off to a good start with four Vodka Martinis, although I'm still not sure why I ordered them as they get me so pissed and don't actually taste that good, especially not with olive juice, which tastes like poisoned ear wax! Maybe I thought they would make me look sophisticated. Again, I don't know why I thought that as she knew everything about me, having watched the last three seasons and she was now living with Caggie.

Halfway through the evening we decided to go for a cigarette and I pulled out the big guns – charming her about the way Shakespeare uses speech. I must stop doing that! But then again, she leant in for a kiss, so maybe not. I reciprocated so enthusiastically I bruised her cheekbone, like a bad blusher accident. I was so excited that I'd finally got with Hattie Clarke I felt like doing Carlton's dance from the *Fresh Prince of Bel Air*, right in the middle of the street.

After the date, we started seeing each other more regularly but it soon became apparent that it wasn't going to be a long-term thing. We are so different from each other it's ridiculous. I finally got to have my romance with Hattie, and realised that it wasn't what I wanted after all.

Not surprisingly people are often interested to know if I get on well with everyone in the *MIC* cast. If I'm being honest, I don't. People are sometimes shocked when I say that, but I see it as no different to any other workplace. If you work in an office you may think that Carol in accounts is a complete asshole – well, it's the same with certain co-stars, if not worse. I don't want to attack anyone in the book, but there are definite personality clashes and it's certainly not one big happy family.

Some people have got egos and at the end of the day all they want is to secure more work, like TV shows and magazine deals, so there are some alpha male characters trying to be cooler than everyone else.

People also like to think that there's some kind of massive rivalry between us and *TOWIE*, but as far as I'm concerned, there really isn't. I get on with all of the cast and have come to know a lot of them quite well. To try to put an end to this rivalry rumour, I suggested that we all shared a table at an awards ceremony and we had an amazing night. I would call people like Joey, Sam, Arg, Gemma, Lydia and Lauren Goodger friends now. And to be quite honest, I would rather spend time with the Essex lot than half the Chelsea lot most of the time. It's great because no one else understands the *MIC* life as well as they do. Reality TV can be quite crazy and of course they're in exactly the same boat as us and they've been through the highs and the lows too.

Cheska once went through a really hard time on the show and felt like she wanted to quit, and she was getting the most awful undeserved abuse on Twitter. She came home one day in floods of tears because someone had tweeted to say that they were going to hunt her down, throw acid in her face and cut her tongue out. It was vile and James 'Arg' Argent called up to check she was OK and said he would always be there if she needed to talk. It just shows you; we are all in this together. Mario showed me how to style my hair after I had it cut, and Lauren

Goodger has stayed in Cheska's bed a few times after nights out in London. We all support each other a lot, and I think the press just like to make up this rivalry.

In fact, I can actually claim to have been in both shows. In September 2012 I somehow managed to do the Virgin Active London triathlon. OK, I'm going to be honest, I did it for the photo call with David Hasselhoff and Richard Branson, not because I wanted to push myself to do a fucking triathlon. It was so much hard work, especially as I had 'forgotten' to train for it (and may have had a couple of Martinis in the days leading up to it). We had to run, cycle and swim, and 15 minutes into the first cycle I thought I was having a cardiac arrest. I was a man who smokes like a chimney and drinks like a fish and hadn't ridden a bike since I was about nine, so I was in real trouble. Finally the bloody thing was over and I did complete it, actually in a good time. I walked over to say goodbye to Lydia, Tom and Debs from *TOWIE*, who had competed in the triathlon too. What I didn't know was that I'd ended up walking onto the bloody *TOWIE* set by mistake. I got a tweet when it was aired from someone saying, 'Did I just see you in the background of *TOWIE*?' Oops!

I don't tend to go to as many parties or events as you may think – my years working on the club scene have beaten it out of me, I guess. In fact I would go as far as to say that I'm starting to become old, something I realised the other day when I walked into HMV in Westfield, straight past the chart music and asked a girl at the desk if she had any Native American pipe music, which is supposed to aid a healthy night's sleep. I suppose I've put my major partying days behind me, but when *Made in Chelsea* was nominated for a BAFTA in 2012 that was not an event I was going to miss.

The show had become incredibly successful worldwide, and by the time Series 2 finished, it was being aired in numerous countries including the United States, Canada and Australia, and in countries like the Congo and the Philippines. My voice is dubbed by someone who sounds nothing like me (I'd love to hear a Filipino say 'Binkletits, darling').

I've heard that it's still the highest downloaded and most tweeted about show that Channel 4 has ever made – apparently there have even been some weeks when we've been tweeted about more than *The X Factor*. The cast and crew put everything into making the show as good as it can be, so it was an honour for that hard work to be recognised with the BAFTA nomination. People do take the piss out of *Chelsea*, but the fact is we aren't actors with lines, we are actually conducting our real lives on camera with over 100 people working behind the scenes 24 hours a day in a huge office in Shoreditch to make the show.

* * *

The BAFTAs was one of the most amazing nights of my life. I'm not usually a big fan of red-carpet events as the photo wall makes my eyebrows sweat and drip into my eye, causing me to look like I have contracted Bell's palsy. Thankfully I didn't do anything stupid that night, like walk up the red carpet with my flies undone. Oh no, wait, I did! We'd been nominated for Best Reality and Constructed Factual, alongside *Don't Tell The Bride*, *An Idiot Abroad* and *The Young Apprentice*. We were in complete disbelief that we'd even been nominated so we never imagined that we could win. *TOWIE* had won the year before, which was voted for by the audiences, but this time it was the BAFTA boards who were deciding whether we should win.

I was asked by the bosses of *Made in Chelsea* whether I minded giving the speech if we won. Of course I said yes, although I sadly didn't get a chance to stand up and accept the award as we lost out to *The Young Apprentice*.

It was an incredible evening and the venue was packed with amazing stars, my favourite being Jennifer Saunders. *Absolutely Fabulous* is comedy genius, and I was so in awe of Jennifer that I virtually stalked her the entire evening, but I didn't have the bollocks to go up and say hello. When later in the evening Jennifer walked past and casually said 'oh hello' to me, I couldn't believe it. Had she caught me stalking her all evening behind the pillars? I was even more astounded when she followed that with 'You're off that *Made in Chelsea*, aren't you?' At this point, I nearly had a little wee in excitement. She went on to say that she didn't watch it but that her daughters love it, and asked for a photo with me. Well, that was worth sweat in the eyes, I assure you. I even said I would be on *Absolutely Fabulous* whenever she was ready to have me, but she smiled and disappeared into the crowds. I then got drunk and snogged a famous actress, but that's another story for another time. Let's just say she never called me back.

When I woke the next morning, I took a step back and tried to look at my life from the outside, to see how crazy it had all become. Five years earlier I had been cleaning up poo in a urinal, but now I was in a TV show that had just been nominated for one of the most esteemed television awards in the world.

It was something I could never have dreamt of when I first interviewed for *MIC* all those years previously. It just shows how your life can change almost overnight when you take a risk.

CHAPTER 22

THE LONG JOHNS AND DUTCH COURAGE

Filming Series 4 was great – I enjoyed everything about it after the emotional rollercoaster of the previous three series. Previously there had been a lot of tension between Gabriella and me, but I finally felt that we had both moved past our break-up, that we'd reconnected on a friendship level, and that we had rediscovered that laughter which had drawn us to each other in the first place. Gabriella and I had a DMC (deep meaningful conversation in boarding school speak), and I told her that I'd never meant to hurt her, which was true: I hadn't. We got everything out in the open once and for all – there had been so many things left unsaid. After that chat, everyone began to speculate about whether we were going to get back together but we didn't know what was going on between us, let alone anyone else. I guess there

was some unfinished business between us somewhere, because before long friendship turned into
flirting. In one episode, we went away to a health spa
and there was definite chemistry between us. To be
honest, I'm surprised that something didn't happen
there, which is why what happened next didn't come
as much of a shock.

I was talking to the *Made in Chelsea* producers over
drinks after filming one day about places I'd like to
visit and I mentioned that I'd never been to
Amsterdam. I was desperate to see what it was like,
and thought it would be a good place to go for
research for this book. The producers agreed that it
would be a great setting for an episode, so when
Gabriella, Cheska, Binky, Richard and I went over
there on holiday for a few days, a small filming crew
accompanied us to the city of sex. We all went out for
dinner and to a nightclub on the first night, where
Gabs and I ended up chatting ... and eventually kissing. It felt completely alien, but at the same time
completely familiar as I remembered her kissing technique. After years of bitterness and hatred it was
strange to be back there again, but on the other hand
it felt completely natural as we had been there so
many times before. Plus we both remembered how
well we worked in bed. We were filming all of the
following day so everyone else wanted to have an
early night. But we were only in Amsterdam for
48 hours – a city I'd been dying to see – so I wanted

to explore. Gabriella felt the same so we ended up necking some wine and heading out to the notorious Red Light District.

We walked down the narrow cobbled streets, saw the prostitutes striking suggestive poses in the windows bathed in a warm red glow, the weed cafés billowing smoke reminding me of the smell of my schooldays. So it seemed like a brilliant idea to get really, really drunk in a bar that I think was called The Grasshopper, but it may well have been named after another insect. Copious amounts of alcohol later and high from passive weed smoking, we ended up back at the hotel – and the two of us in Gabriella's room with a bottle of white wine that we had persuaded reception to sell us. Before long the conversation turned to relationships and we reminisced about how much fun we'd had and how well we'd got on. At this point I'm pretty sure I should have gone back to my room and had a cold shower, but I didn't. There was the unmistakable air of sexual chemistry even though I had been so certain in the past that we would never sleep together again. Though I guess we *were* in the sex capital of the world.

Gabriella decided that she would be more comfortable in her tracksuit bottoms, so she stood up and took off her trousers to show her thong. Why she didn't go and do it in the bathroom, I don't know. Or maybe I do. She bent down to pick the tracksuit bottoms off the floor wearing only her thong, and emboldened by the alcohol I said, 'Why ruin the fun by putting those on?' She smiled her devious smile, jumped onto the bed and said, 'Well, you need to take yours off too.' Amsterdam was incredibly cold so I regret to say I was wearing long johns, which hardly gave a sexy impression when she came to peel them off my legs after a long day of filming. I soon discovered that you can't take off long johns in a sexy fashion! However, they seemed to do the trick and 10 minutes later we were having sex.

We always had amazing sex and that night was no exception. Afterwards, Gabriella felt a post-coital cigarette was needed, and always a gentleman I stumbled down to reception to ask for one, wearing only my long johns, much to the amazement of the poor Dutch woman sitting behind the desk. She kindly and quickly gave me one of hers, I guess to ensure that this drunken British idiot who recited the only Dutch word he knew, *'bloemen'*, which translates directly into the word for flowers (thank you, Ross Geller) would go back to his room before the other guests saw him. We shared the cigarette while looking out of Gabriella's hotel-room window over the Dutch skyline beyond, for which Gabriella received a stern note on her front door the next day warning her that if she did it again she would face a 300 Euro fine. Sorry, Gabs, I'll buy you some *bloemen*.

Weirdly, when I woke up in the morning the first thing I thought wasn't 'Have I honestly just slept with

Gabriella again?' it was, 'Why am I sleeping in long johns and why did I not brush my teeth last night?' It does make me terribly grumpy when I don't floss.

We all spent the day together filming and of course everyone knew what we'd been up to. I assured myself that it wasn't going to happen again, but needless to say that night we did it again … twice. It wasn't ideal and it's not something I would ever make a habit of, but sometimes things happen when you're in the moment and you don't think about the consequences. I don't think you should ever go back to a relationship that hasn't worked because it failed for a reason. After all, I tried with London Girl and it never worked. Unless both of you have changed dramatically you'll still have the same problems (and history) you had before. None of that just magically disappears.

We got back to London and both decided to draw a line under it all – it was closure on both of our parts. That was, without a doubt, the end of the road. We'd never really had closure before so in a way it put an end to a very long, drawn-out chapter.

♥ DEAR OLLIE: THE PERILS ♥ OF CASUAL SEX

Sex absolutely rules the world. However awful it is to imagine, our parents had to have done it at least once. I have an awful feeling that mine were at it like rabbits when I was very young, as I was told over Sunday lunch one day that I was conceived on a sofa on the morning of Ladies' Day at Ascot. What a lovely mental image to keep every time Ascot week comes around.

Sex complicates situations, is a bit of an effort, can be incredibly messy, but above all it feels great in the right circumstances.

You may be interested to know that my magic number at the moment stands at 14, but hopefully I'll manage to push that up by a few before I properly settle down and get married to someone who doesn't mind that my hair will undoubtedly be glossier than theirs.

I'm lucky to have had some incredible relationships, and incredible sex. They always say that sex is so much better when you're with someone you care about. In my opinion, that is bollocks. If men were being honest, they'd agree that the best sex is with a girl they've been seeing for three weeks who is crazy wild in bed and who gives you a very inappropriate blowjob in your car on the way to go and see your mother for

Sunday lunch (now, I'm not saying this has happened to me, of course). In bed she is a porn-star fantasy that a girlfriend could – and should – never be. Can you imagine falling in love with a wild temptress? You'd inevitably find out that she has been shagging your better-hung brother. So while I don't think that sex with someone meaningful is necessarily the most exciting, it is probably better for you in an emotional and physical way. After all, the likelihood is that if they're wild in bed when you barely know them, they're probably quite promiscuous, which is fine if they're always careful but how can you know that for sure?

I just can't understand why someone would put something so precious into something they don't know anything about without any protection. It's like putting your hand into a deep hole in the Indian Ocean – crab territory! I for one am incredibly careful about where I put mini Ollie. It's one of the only things I haven't had cut off, changed its appearance or had pinned back.

But to be honest, I'm not sure I have wild all-night sex in me any more – I like to listen to Radio 4 at night, and I'm only 26! *Desert Island Discs* almost gives me the same feeling as an orgasm when I find out what luxury item the guest would take with them – and you don't even need a smoke afterwards.

Also, another benefit of staying away from random club-night shags is that you avoid the horror of the

Walk of Shame. It's almost a pasttime of mine to drive through Fulham on a Sunday morning to see girls wandering down the King's Road in last night's dress – but without their shoes. You know in an instant what they've been up to – and how much they regret it.

I'll never forget this one time when one of my friends pulled a girl and took her back to his house. She managed to rip her dress during their night of passion, so she was left with nothing to wear home the next day. He still lived with his mother and the only thing he could think to offer her was his younger sister's Disney princess outfit. It was all he was willing to lend to a girl he was clearly never going to see again, so she had no choice but to wear it home. Thankfully she was small enough to fit into it but can you imagine being on the Tube at 9am, trussed up like Cinderella? I'm told she took the wand, told him to fuck off and rocked it!

CHAPTER 23
CAN'T BUY ME LOVE

It's 3 January 2013 and I'm at the end of writing this book. I'm on an 11-hour flight to Mauritius, one of the world's most romantic tropical islands. The hotel has champagne on ice ready for our arrival. Candlelit dinner reservations for two have been made. The honeymoon suite is booked. Everything is perfect. Except one thing – I'm sharing the room with my straight, fireplace-building male friend. However wonderful he is, he's not a girlfriend (we are sleeping in twin beds, I hasten to add). Yes, that's right, 26 years into my quest for true love, and she was proving to be as elusive as ever. Or was she?

At that point, I had been single for a year and a half and although I won't look back on that time with a huge smile on my face and cheer at all the wild sex I didn't have, it enabled me to get to know myself. I always used to laugh at people when they said being single is good for you, as it sounds so pretentious, but I now understand that it's the truth. It made me realise that as much as I wanted to be in a relationship, how could I really get to know some-one else if I didn't know myself yet?

I was recently asked by some friends if I could have any superpower in the world what would it be. Some people replied the ability to fly, others said to be invisible or to be billionaires. I said that all I wanted was a montage of my life set to music that followed all of my relationships so I could watch it back like a film when I'm old and gay – sorry, grey. That's when someone said to me, 'Well, you're already doing that.' I had never thought about the show in that way before. No matter how happy or sad the memory, all of those adventures, those make-ups and break-ups are recorded forever. And now they're written down in this book too.

As I arrived in my honeymoon suite, minus the girl, I took comfort in the knowledge that I still believed in true love. I knew that the right person was out there, and that I would one day find the happiness and contentment I desired. Little did I know that upon my return to a wintery London there would be a girl that would catch my attention. And luckily I caught hers too. Who knows what adventure this story holds, but no doubt you'll watch it happen. I have had 10 incredible girlfriends in 10 incredible years, all of which have shaped and formed the person I am today. I may not always have been lucky in love, but I have what others may desire: a history and great memories.

About a week before Christmas 2012 I got a text message from Tilly's boyfriend, saying that he was planning to ask her to marry him on New Year's Eve. He said he wanted to tell me first as he knew how close we were. I sent my congratulations and told him they were made for each other. It made me think of every moment I had ever spent worrying or crying myself to sleep because I couldn't be with her. I wish someone had told me then that I would not end up with her, so I could have just moved on.

When I think back on my life, I always end up at that night in Southampton, crying on my mother's shoulders about my unrequited love for Tilly before going out to the nightclub where I met Jesters Girl. That evening's events may well have changed my life forever. If I were to give you one lasting piece of advice, it would be simply to take a risk. Because you never know what journey it may take you on, or where you might end up.

So, here's to love – the one thing we can't explain, and the one thing we can't live without.

P.s. Love, if you're out there … hurry the fuck up!

Ollie Locke xx